THE DREAMER WHOU

The Shaman, the Buddha, and the Conscious Dream

THE DREAMER WHO DREAMS YOU

The Shaman, the Buddha, and the Conscious Dream

DANIEL STONE

BOOKS

Winchester, UK
Washington, USA

This book is dedicated to the planet Earth.

Para Arbolita Pashak y Venadito Blanco
Que aprendamos a vivir con amor.

ᒍ ᒉ ᓫ ᒐ ᒡ ᓬ ᒐ ᓭ ᓯ ᓫ ᒐ ᒥ ᓬ ᒐ ᓇ ᒐ ᓬ ᓀ

First published by O-Books, 2012
O-Books is an imprint of John Hunt Publishing Ltd., Laurel House, Station Approach,
Alresford, Hants, SO24 9JH, UK
office1@o-books.net
www.o-books.com

For distributor details and how to order please visit the 'Ordering' section on our website.

ISBN: 978 1 84694 665 3

Design: Arbolita Pashak
Cover paintings: Daniel Stone
Illustrations: Daniel Stone and Arbolita Pashak

Printed in the UK by CPI Antony Rowe
Printed in the USA by Offset Paperback Mfrs, Inc

We operate a distinctive and ethical publishing philosophy in all
areas of our business, from our global network of authors to
production and worldwide distribution.

CONTENTS

INTRODUCTION

A ll my life I have dreamed heavily, and these dreams have always felt more real to me than what most people call 'reality'. As a child I created a private world in which these dreaming dimensions could breathe. Later, I moved the energies into the creative expression – writing, music, painting. I was very sceptical of all things 'spiritual' and accepted my dreamworld more in the context of the 'artist'.

Sixteen years ago, I started a relationship, and I found that sleeping next to my partner, my night dreams went even crazier than ever. I started seeing spirits and forms at night and even during the day. These were the kind of experiences no psychotherapy or psychology could answer. I couldn't paint or write or sing enough to make sense of these dreams. Somewhat in desperation, I had to throw away my spiritual scepticism, because the only beginnings of answers I could feel were in the worlds of what is called the 'occult' or the 'esoteric' – convenient words used to describe what the western rational mind cannot handle. I began to study all kinds of spiritual movements, and was particularly attracted to Wicca. From there my dreams started to talk clearly of 'the shaman'.

It became something of an obsession to find out what this word means. There was a course in Shamanism in North Wales with the Deer Tribe and I thought this course would give me the answers. I learnt a lot, yet there seemed to be something inauthentic in that an Englishman in Wales was translating a tradition from North America devised by someone half Irish and half Cherokee! My dreaming was moving in the right direction, but I still had this yearning to meet the 'real shaman'.

∏ (·) ⋝)(△ ▽ ⊙ ⏚⏛⏐⊣⊢ ⊢ ⊢ ᴕ

My dreaming then told me to go to Peru. When I say 'dreaming', I mean the intuitive messages which we receive day and night. Sometimes these messages can be somewhat obscure, but in this case, I was lying on a beach looking at the stars, and someone from somewhere said – "Go to Peru!" Well, messages are messages, and one can take them or leave them, but when the whole body knows, then the whole body knows, and not to follow such a message would be like denying ones own intuitive innate wisdom held in the bones of the body.

The journey to Peru began a 12-year quest to find the real shaman. In this time, I have worked with shamans in Peru, Bolivia, Australia, Guatemala, Mexico and Nepal.

(I count Tibetan Buddhism as a type of shamanism). I have had many beautiful and mystical experiences, countless ceremonies, teacher plants, theories, stories, myths, and magic. Did I find the real shaman? My question was frustrated by the in-fighting which I found in the shamanic world. It was very rare for me to find a shaman who did not complain about another who was a charlatan because they did not use this type of prayer, or this medicine wheel, or this power tool, or this system from this lineage. I found many shamans in isolated jungles and mountains trying to prove to me that they were the real shamans!

Well, amongst all the squabbling, there were some real jewels. The most authentic shaman I have met was Don

Francisco who lives in the Peruvian Amazon. He runs retreats working with curative plants. His whole manner is beautifully simple. Very little ceremony, very little ritual, a short prayer, a blow of tobacco over the plant mixture, and a song. He drinks, we drink, and then the song. Sometimes the song lasts a few minutes, sometimes the whole night. The song leads the dreamer through the dreams of the earth, the dreams of other worlds, other dimensions. I have heard many songs used by shamans to communicate with the spirit world, but this song, more than any other, went straight to the heart. There was no need for elaborate ceremony, theory, or ritual. The song did what the Dzogchen Tibetan Buddhists call – 'Cutting Through'. His song went directly to the heart of matter.

$$\Pi\ (\cdot)\ \lesssim)(\ \triangle\ \triangledown\ \odot\ \omega/\dashv\ \mathsf{h}\ \mathsf{H}\ \alpha$$

Who can teach this? Who can teach how to open the heart? I used the word 'authentic' to describe this shaman because something was touched deeply inside of me. What moved me was song, which was not his song. It was the song of the jungle, of the plants, of the trees that sang through him. This shaman was invisible – I could forget him and listen to the voices of the planet earth. My authentic real shaman did not exist. Supreme humility was his beauty.

This meeting with Don Francisco changed the scope of the enquiry. I had met someone I could truly say felt like a real shaman to me, yet my question did not feel answered. I had met the real shaman and yet I was still looking for the real shaman. My dreaming took me to Thailand and Nepal and a long and deep enquiry into my connection with the Buddhist tradition. I studied in the Buddhist temples and came up with a similar question - who is the real Shaman - who is the real Buddha?

There was still something intangible which was missing. I had to let this contradiction hang in the air for a while, without really understanding it. I realised I did not understand the question. So, trying to understand the question, I was taken to Mexico. I was following one of those messages that you can't argue with. The message was just as blunt – "Go to Mexico" – which was somewhat inconvenient at the time because I was in the Bolivian Amazon. However, I was far enough down the path of following the intuitive messages to know that I may not know the meaning of the message until later. I had no idea about Mexico and it was the first of the 30 countries I have visited without a guidebook. I didn't need one. This was home. Home in the bones. A resonance I had never felt before anywhere in the world. Mexico had called me.

Continuing my 'real shaman' question, I set up a meeting with the Huichol shamans in the north. It was and is very difficult to connect with the isolated Huichols. It required a lot of 'luck' and work and patience over a period of a year to arrange it. Because of all this effort, by the time it was set up, it felt very precious. You get out what you put in. I met the young Huichol with whom I was to wait for the shaman or 'curandero' or 'maracami', in Morelia, Central Mexico. We had to wait some days, and on one of these days, I sat in a café overlooking the central plaza. I heard a voice that basically said – "Go to the desert by yourself". I had a furious argument with this voice because of all the work I had put in, but the voice just repeated itself. These voices don't use reason; they are more like energies, impulses. It is a bit like trying to argue with your own God. Well, if Woody Allen does it, why not me? Just for the record, God won and I went to the desert by myself.

ᴦᴑʃⱧᴦᴦⱧᴦⱧᴦⱧ—)(ꙩᴦᴦᴑ7ⱧᴦꞮ7Ⱨ 6 ᴧᴦ 7ꙩ

If shamans had taught me anything, it is how to listen to the Earth. They have taught me how to listen to the stars, the planets. The most important lesson I have learnt from them is that everything speaks, everything has a language – the trees, the plants, the rocks, the rivers, the mountains, the sea. It is just a question of learning languages. In the desert, this lesson came home to me more than ever. Lying in the Earth, I could feel how it breathes through my body, how the stars connect through the breath, and how the tree is an intermediary between dimensions. It was here that I understood why I was told to come alone. The real shaman was not a man who does not speak my language, whose customs and traditions are so far from my own. The real shaman was inside of me. I could hear him talking directly, showing me new ways to listen to new languages, how to walk calmly between the worlds, between dreams. I could feel this shaman as intimately as a lover, as real as love, as honest as nakedness. This shaman could speak straight from the heart.

Am I so special? No. The artist, the poet, the priest, the priestess, the healer, the magician, the counsellor, the lover. These are the compositions of the 'real shaman' inside waiting to be sung.

Some years later, I was told by my guides to meet with the Huichols again. This time there was clarity around what is possible in such a relation and what is not. As the Huichol shaman sang, I understood that the indigenous shamans sing the song of the land in which they live. They have a continuous dialogue. It is a dialogue between the human and the other beings on this planet. It is also a dialogue with other planets and the stars. This song has been sung for centuries. The preciousness of their song is our connection with this life. When it is lost, we will lose a part of ourselves. The Huichol shaman sang, and I listened to the land that he sings.

What the Huichol shaman cannot do so well is to bridge the huge gap between cultures, between traditions and times. For this, there is a need for translators, time travellers who can more between these worlds on the earth from the desert and the jungle to the city. Even within Mexico, translators are needed to bridge the gap between the indigenous cultures and the modern city life. They are worlds that don't understand each other's language. The city roars, but without the wisdom of the root.

I could go back to my teacher in North Wales I hope with a touch more humility. He also was a translator, trying to help us remember the root of our ancestral knowledge. He helped me on the path of opening my heart to the memory. Was he a real shaman? Well, I can say now with all the incredible lightness of being – it doesn't matter.

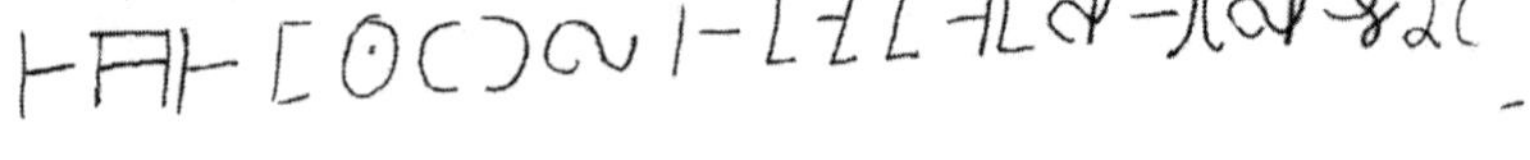

This book has been written over a period of seven years under the supervision of my most influential teacher – Chu-Ra, who lives in Mexico. It developed from a writing relation with the desert, which culminated in a piece of writing that seemed to bring together the essence of all the teachings I have received from around the world. This is printed in full in the chapter 'Speak'. I took the piece to Chu-Ra, and she told me that it needed translation. There then followed a six-year period of careful translation which has gone through many trials and errors with circles and seminars. I understand that my work is linguistic in the sense of translating languages between worlds, and so much of the work is in trying to feel the right sound, the song.

A small section of 'speak' is given at the beginning of each chapter in italic. I then offer a theoretical framework, particularly in the earlier chapters, together with personal experiences. Exercises are also given. They are designed to be building blocks, which develop the strength of the reader's ability to dream the day and the night with full consciousness. The experiences in the desert taught me, more than anything, that the greatest teachers are all around us and inside us. They are waiting for the opportunity to be heard. When the space is made, there is a chance to listen.

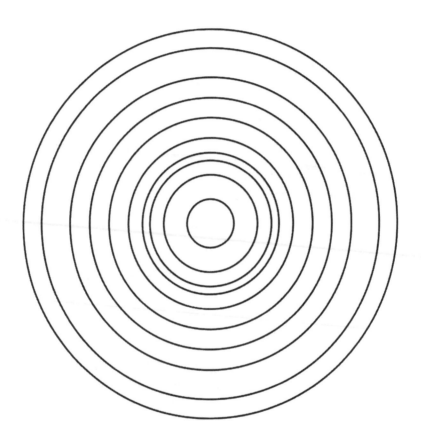

ONE - BREATH

We start at the beginning. First breath. Without intention. An exhalation. No thought. By itself. It began. Breath of no thing. Natural. Nothing itself. There is no difference.

An inhalation. Appearing different. From no breath to breath. But there was no intention. It was nothing. It still is nothing.

And then the catch.

Everything comes from nothing

I remember one moment at university that changed the course of my life. I was on the way to the first lecture of the morning. I walked down the same road I had walked down for over a year. There was nothing apparently extraordinary about that morning, my mind was wandering in its own way, and then it stopped. My mind stopped. My stomach left me. It was like those cartoons where the character is running over land and carries on running over a cliff. There is that classic moment when the character realises that there is nothing underneath. No more land on which to run. This is the point where the character looks into the camera at the viewer in desperation.

I looked at the house. I looked at the people around me. I could no longer believe in them. I could no longer believe they existed. Everyone was walking as if they knew what they were doing and where they were going. In this moment I knew they had no idea. I had no idea. We were all going through the motions. The world became a stage-set with actors unaware that they were acting. I couldn't move. I could hardly breathe.

> I was staring one enormous question in the face –
> What is real?
> And the only answer I could feel was –
> Nothing.

Everything comes from nothing. I understood in this moment this excruciating and exhilarating paradox. My stomach left me. In its place was fear. Anxiety. Dread. And then it changed to something that seemed even bigger. Love. Bigger than love. A completion. In my breath, there was something that wasn't breathing. My breath was something and nothing at the same time.

The moment came and went. I continued walking in a stupor. I went to the lecture and stared the whole time at the clouds. Something had changed. I wasn't the same. I found it difficult to study and soon left university. I tried to understand this moment for many years, but it was only when I began to meditate, some years later, that I could begin to make some sense of this 'something coming from nothing.' The nothing is not the nothing of negation. It is the nothing of everything. The Buddhist teachers I have met call it the Dharmakaya. Quabbalist teachers have called it the Ain Soph. The individual no longer needs to exist in separation, and becomes instead the all. The First Breath is the thinnest line on the horizon between the all and the nothing.

Completion asks for nothing because it is complete. The breath is given without any expectation. It is unconditional. There are places we can reach through the breath where everything is given for nothing. It is our root. Our birthright. We were born free.

The Great Mystery of the universe is – why the universe? Why was there a movement from completion to separation? No one knows (that is why it is a mystery), but lots of people have fun trying to guess. There are a lot of clues - what moves a painter to paint a picture; what moves a writer to write a book; what moves a filmmaker to make a film; a poet to sing? The Australian Aboriginals believe that the Earth is a perfect dream that flows from and with the stars. The dreamer is the artist and the dreamed Earth the masterpiece. The breath of the universe is the continuing dream. We are part of a painting which is being painted whilst we breathe.

To touch the First Breath is to touch the edge of the creative mind. It is the place where the painter is the painted, the writer the written, the poet the song, the dreamer is the dreamt. When a meditator reaches the profound depths of the breath, the paradoxes do not create tension. There are places in the breath where there is nothing to be explained.

Breath Awareness Meditations

Breath awareness meditations are easy and difficult. They are easy because all we are required to do is to sit and breathe. They are difficult because most people don't know how to simply sit and breathe.

Why is this?

Most people lead very busy lives, externally, internally, or both. The mind becomes very congested. Busy minded people are constantly followed by trains of thought. When they stop to simply breathe, the trains catch up, and the mind is buzzing like Waterloo station at peak hours. This is when the war begins –

"This isn't meditation, this is hell."

"I'm useless at meditating."

"I need a drink."

The mistake I made when I assiduously tried to study meditation, was the mistake everyone seems to make – trying too hard. I went from temple to temple in Asia looking for that moment when I could say I had a good meditation. I judged which was a right thought and which a wrong thought, and so ended up in a state of constant reaction to my experience. The point of breath awareness meditation is not to have a particular thought or feeling or sensation, but to become aware of what the thoughts and feelings and sensations are. Our busy minds cloud our deeper sensations, feelings and thoughts, both pleasurable and painful. Breath meditations deepen our level of experience.

Many people get stuck in the war stage because they have an immediate expectation that meditation should be comfortable and enjoyable, even light and fluffy. There is an attempt to grasp at a particular experience. Breath awareness meditations are designed to raise ones awareness of what is going on in the mind. It may be hell; it may be heaven. It may be undramatic, even boring. It depends on your truth in the moment of the breath.

The war stage may last five minutes or fifty. Usually, for most people, it calms down with the natural flow of breath. Nothing stays the same forever. The natural breath is the tool to quieten the busy mind. When the mind is quiet, there is insight. Sand in the desert is picked up by the wind, and when the wind passes, the sand gradually settles back into the Earth. The vision opens by degrees, through war and peace, and the mysteries in the breath of the universe are revealed.

Exercise 1. **The Practise of Meditation**

Before meditating, it is useful to find a space in a room that is specifically for this purpose. Turn off the phone and if necessary put a note on your door – "Do not disturb!" This is your time. It helps to make some kind of altar. A candle, water, and incense are the basics. Also precious stones and any objects which are sacred to you would help to make this place special in your life.

To find a good sitting position is an exercise in itself. It helps to experiment. Sitting on the floor cross-legged with the spine slightly raised is a classic position. Sitting on the knees with cushions raising the spine is another well-used position. Sitting on a chair or with the back against the wall will also serve well. The two general principles are that the spine should be erect and that you are reasonably comfortable.

When you are ready, close your eyes and breathe naturally. Stay with the breath, your natural breath. It is likely that your mind will wander. When you become aware of this, don't beat yourself up about it. Simply return yourself gently to the breath. Your natural breath. Whatever you think, whatever you feel, is just your truth in the moment. It is neither good nor bad. The beauty of the breath can be experienced in its fullest when there is acceptance.

If you have never meditated before, fifteen minutes a day would be a good start. When you feel ready, increase to twice a day. Then to twenty minutes, half an hour, forty minutes and so on. An hour-long meditation is very powerful and is worth aiming for, but not essential. You will find what is the right timing for you. Patience, in these meditations, is THE virtue. Consistency and perseverance will give the breath a chance to teach you what you already know. In the breath is the memory of all the knowledge you hold in your self.

Exercise 2. **Breath Awareness Movement Meditation**

Movement meditations take the experience of the sitting meditations more profoundly into the physical experience. They can make more sense of the sitting meditations and can interpret an often abstract experience into an experience that feels more grounded and present in the physical body.

First of all find a good position for your feet on the floor. Experiment to find a solid relation between your physical presence and the physical presence of the planet on which you walk.

When you have found a firm connection, move your body very gently from one side to the other. Allow yourself to feel the natural rhythm of your body's movement. When the rhythm feels steady and settled, co-ordinate the movement with your breath. Your natural breath. This could be an inhalation one side and an exhalation on the other; or an inhalation and exhalation on one side, and an inhalation and exhalation on the other.

Experiment with all the options:

LEFT SIDE	RIGHT SIDE
Inhalation	Exhalation
Exhalation	Inhalation
Inhalation and exhalation	Inhalation and exhalation

When you have found the combination that suits you, allow your body to move your breath and allow your breath to move your body. As this meditation deepens, the body becomes the breath and the breath becomes the body.

The breath is our home in this work. If you are following this course by yourself, I suggest taking at least a month listening to the breath before proceeding to the next step. In later exercises you will need to know your breath very well so that you can orientate yourself in your body on Earth. Through the breath you can travel through the whole dream of the universe, and through the breath you can just as easily return.

TWO - FORM

And then the catch. This energy. To catch the energy of the first breath. And make something. The designers. The dreamers. To take this energy – entirely nothing, entirely free of intention – and use it for something. The possibilities are endless. What would it be like?

The dreamers. They came after the initial breath. They came from the breath. But they were different from the pure breath. Because they had intention. They had big ideas. Plans. The original breath is free of care. It does not have any intention. It is the essence of nothing. But the dreamers want to make something of it.

What were the first experiments? Half forms. Playing. Appearance and disappearance. A hint of a possibility. Shapes that never quite stick, fluidity; a stream of the consciousness of beginnings. The magicians starting from scratch.

What do they learn? Light and darkness. Two tones. The one makes the other. Difference. And space. Continuum. Limitation. Boundary. Form.

To keep the image still, they have to concentrate. To hold something in place requires focus. The dreamers learn how to make a decision. They discover time.

This is it. Even if it is for a second. A form needs time to exist, or it is lost in the continuum. The more time that is given to the form, the more fixed it can become. The dreamers have to learn to focus. And then they can make something. Even if it is only for a second.

Concept of time. Concept of space. Concept of difference. These are the basic starting places of the magicians. And then they get clever. They discover the differences in light. They discover colour. They discover differences in darkness. They discover depth. Perspective. Spaces within spaces. And then the masterstroke. Volume. . The possibility of the third dimension. The object. The object in perspective..

Life is a dream

The moment when the illusion is shattered is a shock. I remember the confusion that followed the moment I stopped on the way to the university lecture. I no longer knew in what to believe. Not only did the 'education' I was receiving become irrelevant - everything seemed irrelevant. I couldn't connect with conversation, I could no longer connect easily with the context in which the people around me were living. I found more answers in the silence.

Many people who find themselves attracted to this kind of work, have somewhere along the line received a shock in their life. A relationship ends, someone dies, they lose their job, a physical injury, a very strong dream, a 'mystical' experience. Something happens which changes the way they look at reality.

Our education system tends to focus on the material reality, as if the material reality is the only reality. When that is shown to be a lie, one is left floundering. One illusion falls, and the others follow in quick succession like a house of cards. It becomes clear how much is taken for granted. A deeper sensitivity emerges. Other energies become more apparent. Feelings. Intuitions. Hunches that can no longer be ignored.

There have been many experienced elders who have tried to teach me how to make clear sense of the world since that first 'shock', yet the most accurate was a fellow student, a Mexican man, sixteen years my junior, called Jonas. He showed me a very simple experience, which in a way interpreted what the elders had been trying to get through to me.

Jonas took me to a park on the outskirts of Mexico City. We sat against a tree. The exercise was to look at one point on another tree in front me. The back of Jonas's head was about 45 degrees from mine. Jonas had a way of talking through the back of his head. There are many teachers, particularly in Mexico, who do this. What they project into the world, their face, is a tiny fraction of who they are. The mask is very popular in Mexican culture. In their ceremonies and processions, a spirit being – like a very strong characteristic – is exaggerated into bizarre faces. In 'The labyrinth of solitude' Octavio Paz explains how this projection of the mask is so much a part of the way in which Mexicans see themselves. Masks. Phantoms. They know that most of what is expressed is not real. It is a projection. The strongest energy is behind, unseen on the surface. The secrets of the Mexicans are only revealed through the 'second sight' - seeing behind.

I started to do the exercise, focusing on one point on the tree, and trying to open my own second sight. I stared at the point for some time. After a while the point in the tree took me into a dream. I felt as though I was dreaming. I felt as if my physical body was asleep. I came out of the point and saw the tree as if I was dreaming it. On the outside, nothing physically had changed. I was still on the ground, leaning against a tree, looking in the same direction. The difference was that I was looking at the tree as if the tree was being dreamed. I went again into the point. After a while, colours and sounds evolved. The colours were related to the sounds. I couldn't understand the sounds in words through my intellect, but I knew that the tree was communicating to me in some way. I came out of the tree and I understood more than ever before, that as much as I was dreaming the tree, the tree was dreaming me. I laughed out loud as if it was the biggest joke in the whole wide world.

"What happened?" said Jonas.

"Everything is as it should be," I said. I felt an immense sense of peace.

The initial movement into the sense that I was dreaming a tree opened up in me many layers of sensitivity. The five well-known senses were heightened, but also there was something else, another layer of sensitivity. I have often had dreams at night when I become aware that I am dreaming. These moments of awareness within the dream are precious. There is an excitement. Possibility. My perspective changes from watching a film in which I am a participant, to becoming a co-creator of that film. The dream is no longer only happening to me – I become responsible for making the dream happen. I have choice in the development of my own dream. Great. This is when I usually start to fly! I love flying in dreams, and each time I have the opportunity to fly, I try something new, like backward somersaults, controlling the speed of the flight, direction, altitude. Learning each time to fly my own plane. Freedom.

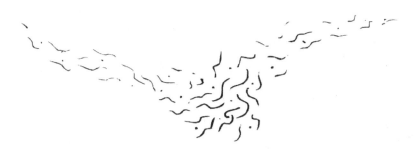

Freedom. The moment the tree became a subject of my dream, there was the same possibility. The doors of perception opened. There was something different about this experience. Something new. I went back into the point for more information. The tree returned my gaze. It showed ma its consciousness. This turned everything round. I love trees, I have found wisdom in them, and the idea that a tree was dreaming me felt very consoling.

"It is time to go," said Jonas.

From the tree in the park, Jonas took me into the city. Mexico City is one of the loudest, crudest, most polluted cities in the world. It didn't take long for my peace to be shattered. From being so open, I felt like my energies were being assaulted by a blindly insensitive world, and as the saying goes, I wanted to get off! We were travelling in a very crowded underground train. I felt this must be pretty close to hell. Jonas told me to focus on one point. Any point. I took my attention to one point and fixed my attention on it. Gradually, as my attention stabilised, I began to remember the peace I had felt with the tree. Many people came and went in the chaos of the peak time tube travelling through the city centre, but I found myself forgetting their stress and forgetting my stress. My fixed attention held my dream in the chaos.

Thought - vibrations

The First Breath contains an immense charge of energy. This charge comes from the phenomenal effort it takes to move into separation. Completion has to think into parts of itself. One Mind becomes thought. Pure thought. It is inspiration, an enormous gush in all directions, everywhere. It is like a ubiquitous multi-directional hurricane and it sets up a charge of unimaginable force and power. The charge is an intense vibration. The vibration is between thought and the thinker. It is a creative tension. The tension creates fire. From this creative fire is born the dreamer and the dream.

The first Breath is an infinite opportunity. The exhalation and the inhalation present the dreamers with the simplest basis of all existence: the law of opposites. For nothing to exist there must be something; for there to be timelessness there must be time; for there to be completion there must be incompletion; for there to be a thinker, there must be thought. The creation within One Mind of the thinker and thought, made the law of opposites possible. Within every conception has to be the opposite of the conception.

The law of opposites is beautifully illustrated in the yin-yang sign:

The white within the black makes the black; the black within the white makes the white. Without the other, neither could be identified.

From the opposition of thinker and thought came the dreamer and dreamed. There is One Mind, but there is not one dreamer. There are dreamers. The transformation from the One Mind to the many dreamers is the creation of time.

Dreamers slow down the energy of the mind. They slow down the thought-vibrations. The dreamers go into the light source – thought – and slow the energy down by focusing on one part. By dividing all of time (timelessness) and all of space (infinity), they make **some** time and **some** space. This is workable. The dreamer can then use the energy of the thinker like the film projectionist uses light to project the film. The thinker is the light. Time and space the screen. The dreamer is the filmmaker, a filmmaker who doesn't completely understand the energy of the film. It can never be entirely controlled.

The dream is dreamt by sustaining attention. This is the holding of the image in time and space. The dreamers had to learn to direct and control the energy of the creative fire. In essence, this uses the same principle as the energy of the First Breath. The creative tension between the thinker and the thought, becomes the creative tension between the dreamer and the dreamt. It is a further act of separation within the mind, and within this creative tension is the magic that creates the universe. The magic can be described in four stages.

The dreamer intends to see.

The dreamer projects the focus of the eyes like a long lens camera.

The dreamer sees.

The dreamer has to relax the attention.

My Mexican teachers call the dreamer's magic trick of being both the viewer and the viewed, the Time Circle of Seeing.

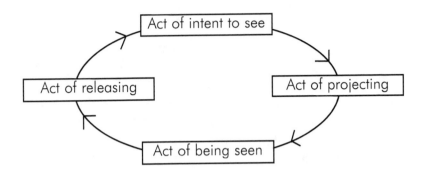

The act of seeing is the opening of the dreamer's 'eyes'. The dreamer's eyes are like filters, which control how much light is allowed to be directed into the space.

The act of projection is the process of design.

The act of being seen is the holding of the object in time and space.

The act of releasing is the relief from the effort of attention and also the necessity to blink. The act of releasing has to occur because the effort needed to sustain attention within the creative fire of thought vibration – even for a millisecond – is enormous. The partial closing of the eyes controls the light. If the dreamers' eyes were always completely open, the dream would be swamped with the wave of random movement - pure thought – and no image could be sustained. To sustain attention requires the skilful use of opening and closing the eyes. The dreamer closes the eyes and looks again. This sets up a time circle, which holds the image in place.

If you flick through the corners of the pages in this chapter, you will see the repetition of the same image. The dreamer holds time in space by continuously repeating the same circle of attention – opening and closing the eyes. Because of the phenomenal force behind the First Breath, even to hold a dot in space in time would have taken aeons of fixed attention to achieve.

The idea that the universe is made of thought vibration is a very old idea. It is the foundation of the Buddhist 'science of the mind'. The idea of the dreamers being the designers of the universe comes from the Australian Aboriginal perspective as well as the shamanic traditions of the Americas. Dreamers are the magicians who spin the cosmic web. The cosmic web is the thread between all the realities in the One Mind. The initial dreamers were in touch with the first breath to the extent that they were able to see everything in the context of the whole. But as the process of separation developed – the dreams within dreams within dreams – the perspective of the One Mind was lost. It is the belief of almost every elder and teacher I have met, that the human dream has lost contact with the rest, and this is the root of human loneliness – the isolated dream.

I return to the moment when I understood that the tree was dreaming me. It touched me. I felt within me deep peace. Home. I realised in that moment that I am not alone. I do not dream in isolation. I was being guided by a sense of knowledge and wisdom that was far deeper than what I had believed 'humanity' to be. If I was being dreamed, then I wanted to know the mind that dreams me. I wanted to look deeper into the universe.

The One-point Meditation

Sitting on the Earth looking at a rock. There is no breeze, the sky is clear. Sitting in your room looking at the wall. There is no one around, the phone doesn't ring. It all appears very silent, very still.

At the same time, the great Teutonic plates on the Earth's surface are shifting and even the mountains move; the Earth moves around the Sun and is spinning very fast on its own axis; the Earth and the Sun together with all the other planets in the solar system are moving within the galaxy; the galaxy shifts the great universal shuffle; the blood of the universe is being pumped by your heart around your whole body - and somehow the wall stays still, the sky is clear, the rock doesn't seem to have moved an inch!

We live in this constant illusion, as if everything is fixed, everything secure. A rock is a rock, a spade a spade. This is the work of aeons of focused dreaming. The dreamers have mastered the art of fixed attention with such incredible impeccability; it is hard for us to believe that the root of it all is the free form of random movement.

Consider your own dream, and how your dream is influenced by the dreams of others: the dream of your mother; the dream of your father; dreams of your brothers, sisters, your friends, partners, lovers, teachers; dream of the school, college, colleagues, neighbours; dream of your boss, your government; television dreams, newspapers, radio, theatre, film, books; dream of the whole of your culture, your nation state; the dreams of this century, dreams of previous centuries. Dream of the Earth. Dream of the solar system. Dream of the galaxy. Dream of the universe.

So many dreams and so many dreamers trying to influence you, it is a wonder you can remember anything at all.

For all these reasons, the one-point meditation is phenomenally difficult, but not impossible. It is the first step in training yourself to be conscious in your own dream. Almost everyone is unconscious of the forces that dream him or her. They are like walk-on extras in a film who are only told what to do for their specific moment in the crowd scene, and are not shown the rest of the script. The conscious dreamer moves towards an awareness which not only shows them the script of the film in which they are acting, but also the script-writer, musicians, costume designer, stage manager and promoter. The conscious dreamer actually becomes the co-writer and co-creator of their own dream.

Exercise 3. **One-point Meditation Practise**

This meditation starts with the breath awareness meditation of the first chapter.

After about ten minutes, focus on a point on the wall or an object in front of you. The distance need not be exact. In fact you can experiment with distance. It should be near enough for you to be able to see the point clearly. Keep your attention fixed on that point for at least fifteen minutes. This will help you to stabilise your breath and your attention so that you become less distracted.

Now close your eyes. Focus on a point inside your vision. This is more difficult. Your mind will move all over the place. See if you can return to the same spot and hold your attention on that point. Be patient with your self. This isn't easy. With practise you will begin to learn how to fix your attention.

The Triangle

In the Hindu Yantric tradition the universe begins with one point which is called the Bindu. Then the creator-dancer Shiva stretches out his arm in a line. The line finds a second point, Shakti. Together they find the third point in the universe, their creation. The result is the first solid form. The triangle.

The triangle is a kind of building block. It is considered to be one of the finest thought vibrations since so much can be made with it. The yantras are beautiful designs that use the triangle as the basic shape. The famous Sri-yantra is a woven pattern of triangles with upside down triangles inside. It is a very sophisticated focus of meditation.

Sri-Yantra

The triangle is associated with the Hara or the second chakra. This is the power centre of the energetic body, which is above the groin and below the navel. The triangle helps us to connect with our power centre. In the phenomenal throught-vibrations of the universal dream, we need all the power we have to simply survive, never alone be active. The triangle is a visual and actual energetic source of power in the dream.

The breath, the one-point and the triangle. These are the roots and our gateway to the dream of the universe. When we are sure of our breath and sure of the point of our power, there is no chance of getting lost. We are ready to travel.

Exercise 4. **Triangle Meditation Practise**

This meditation begins with the breath awareness meditation and the one-point meditation. After you have closed your eyes and focused on a point inside, begin to draw the lines of the creator-dancer Shiva. Dream your own triangle, and then hold the attention on this shape. This will create a two-dimensional image.

Try then to extend the image into a three dimensional projection by focusing on a pyramid. It may also help to put your hand on the second chakra area.

The triangle meditation is particularly useful if you feel spun out and vulnerable. I use it a lot in chaotic cities like Lima just to stay focused. A particularly potent meditation is on the bindu in the middle of a triangle whilst focusing on the second chakra.

These exercises are very portable. If you don't get to do them in the morning, you can do them on the train. On the plane. On your bike. In the rain. You could also do them in the afternoon, or at night. There are fixed points all the time, everywhere. There is also breath everywhere, unless you are physically dead, in which case I would like to meet you.

The breath and the triangle. These are the two roots and our gateway to the dream of the universe. When we are sure of our breath and sure of the point of our power, there is no chance of getting lost. We are ready to travel.

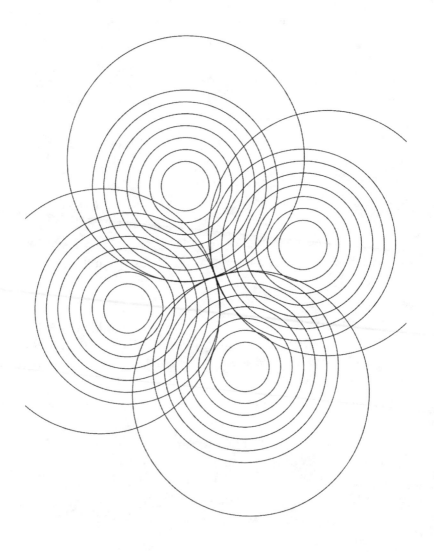

THREE - THE ELEMENTS

The dreamers wanted to make something that matters, something more than just an idea and a possibility. They discovered the elements. Still from the same original breath. They discovered how to transform breath into air, the speed of air into fire, then hot slowing to cold. The formation of gases. Gas can congest into rock or condense into water. It was a magical time. The dreamers made huge discoveries. And all from the breath of nothing. They couldn't believe their luck.

Space, time, light, shadow, the third dimension and now the elements. The experiments really could begin. They worked with extremes at first, extremes of fire, extremes of earth; they made planets and stars over and again, practising with various gradients of the elements, but to a large extent they did not know what they were doing, they did and do not have complete control. The first breath from nothing was unconditional, and so had no control over the designers who used the breath. Those same dreamer designers at this stage have little control over their designs. The elements are such big principles; they have a sense of their own law, which the dreamers understood in theory but not in practise. Each star and each planet was the attempt by the dreamers to get a clearer idea of how the elements actually work. In time, they learnt, and so these novice chemists and physicists begin to develop the possibility of balance. It was all about focus again. By holding planets in certain rotations they could create fields of energy that would remain in place. It is like creating a context, or a background, and they found a way to hold their focus long enough to explore further possibilities. So in our solar system, for example, the dreamers are holding the focus of planets orbiting one central star. This has the effect of creating various fields of energy, which have a certain consistency in which other life forms can thrive. This system of our star sun was by no means the first with which the dreamers developed this type of attention. It is an idea that they had been developing through many repetitions and each repetition in infinity gave them a chance to perfect their idea.

The planets and stars were like the stage set of the dreamers' play. They developed through numerous design stages an elemental principle that enabled them to experiment with various forms. Their first experiments were very simple and kept very close to the essence of the four essential elements. But as they developed their skills, they could make increasingly complex creatures and on a planet such as Earth, which was one of their better constructions, they could play with all kinds of ideas.

All forms are made of a combination of air, fire, earth, and water

The illusion is shattered. The material world no longer holds so true, and the question still rings in the ear –
What is real?

In a sense, the moment when the illusion is seen has the effect of stripping everything away. It leaves one naked, with nothing. This is a great place to start.

I have always been attracted to deserts. The first desert I saw was in Mongolia. I was riding the Trans-Siberian Express from Moscow to Peking. Riding on the train through the Mongolian plains, something leapt out of me. I couldn't keep my eyes off the land even though there was nothing to keep my eyes on! Space.

Close to Ulan Bator, the Mongolian capital, the track sizes change and so you have to get out of one train and get into another. I was allowed to get off the train for half an hour. I stared into the Mongolian desert and I learnt more in that half-hour, it felt, than the whole of what had gone before. Truth, at last. Nothing. Everything and nothing. My body knew something, something so powerful, it cannot be denied.

Fifteen years later I was in the Sonora desert, Mexico. A teacher (who cannot be named) took me to the desert. After several hours walking, he stopped. He told me to take off my clothes.

"Stay as you are," he said, and left me there.

In those moments in the desert I knew what it was like when the stomach left me, the moment I stopped and the illusions fell away. Naked, in the middle of nowhere. In the desert that day I went through the same anxiety and the same elation. It felt like an end and a beginning. From here, from the reality of nothingness, I was to re-enter the material world as it is. Not a fixed reality, but something dreamed. Something transitory. Something made of pure magic.

The elements are the magic tricks of the dreamers that make the material reality. They wanted to make something more than an idea or a possibility, like a building is more than the architect's design. It becomes more apparently real. Fixed.

The Elemental Circle

The four elements are different types of attention, which relate to the Circle of Seeing:

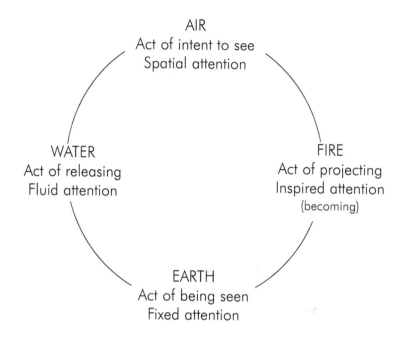

CIRCLE OF SEEING

Air is the element that connects one dream with all the other dreams. It is awareness of space and interconnection. Air is nearest to completion and wholeness. It is the beginning of separation, thinker and thought, space within mind, the white canvas.

Fire is the inspiration, the quickening of Air. It is like an atomic friction, a very fast vibration. The creative tension is between the dreamer attempting to control time and space, and the random movement of pure thought.

Earth is the control of the image. The strength of the control depends on the level of sustained attention.

Earth is only possible because the element of Water slows down the vibration of inspired Fire. The coolly inspired artist. Earth is a balance between the inspiration (quickening), and the releasing (slowing down).

The Medicine Wheel

The medicine wheel is a very ancient technique to balance the four elements in ourselves. The basic principle is that when the four elements are balanced, we have good health in body, mind and spirit. When the elements are out of balance, we become ill in some way.

The medicine wheel is also a way of orientating ourselves on the land. Each element is assigned to the four cardinal directions. These four elemental spirits hold the ceremonial space.

There are various types of medicine wheel. The first wheel I learnt when studying Wicca. It is the Celtic medicine wheel.

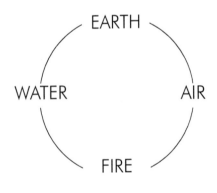

CELTIC MEDICINE WHEEL

I then studied with the North American shamanic wheel used by many tribes in the U.S. and Canada.

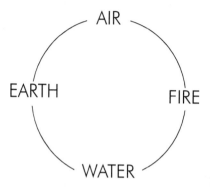

NORTH AMERICAN SHAMANIC MEDICINE WHEEL

I then travelled to work with shamans in South America, Asia and Australia and discovered various forms of wheels. They were not all called medicine wheels, but they functioned for the same purpose: balance. This left me rather confused and I didn't know which medicine wheel to work with. For three years whilst travelling more and studying, I experimented with every possible combination of medicine wheel to find my definitive version. It was extraordinary to discover that some days Air was definitely in the North and other days it was definitely in the South! However, I settled finally on this medicine wheel:

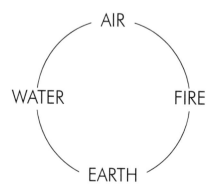

The reasons were mainly to do with the way in which energy moves into and out of the Earth. Air is closest to the breath; it is the element that comes before formation. Fire is the projection, the movement of Air through space. Earth is the slowing down of fire into form. Water is the element of transformation back to Air. It is a circle, like the breath, and when the circle finds a good rhythm, it flows very well.

I worked with this medicine wheel on my own and with groups, thinking this was my own peculiar discovery, and I tended to advise people that they may discover (after a lot of experimentation) a medicine wheel that was more suitable for them. Then in Mexico, when I was teaching a group with Ea Orgu, who works in the Mayan tradition, he informed me that I was working with the Mayan medicine wheel. I have been more attracted to work in Mexico than any other country, and this for me, was a formal reassurance. Working with the Mayan medicine wheel has always been the centre of my work with groups. The intuitive approach to feeling the dream had shown me where I am supposed to be, and the right form for me to use.

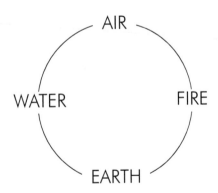

THE MAYAN MEDICINE WHEEL

Exercise 5. **The Medicine Wheel Exercise**

The first step is to find a spot. This is an exercise in itself because it requires us to open our intuition to the land and feel. The right place is just known to the body and the body opens until it finds it. There may be signs which help, a particular tree, an animal, a flower, a rock. It is not something that has to be thought, because after a while, we always arrive at the place where we are supposed to be. The body knows.

When you have found your spot, orientate yourself either by looking at the sun and knowing its movement, or by using a compass. Then walk in the direction of the North in order to find a stone or rock. This stone is the stone that will mark the place of Air in the medicine wheel. Finding a stone is another exercise in itself. Again we are opening our intuition to feel which stone is the right stone. It will just feel right. Lift the stone to the sun and then bring it to your heart, asking that this stone speaks to you through the element of Air. The Sun is our star and our connection with our ancestors, the ancient dreamers who hold the keys of wisdom. Then, returning to your spot, place the stone at the North.

Moving then to the East, walk to find the stone of Fire, to the South the stone of Earth and to the West the stone of Water. Bring these back to your spot and mark out the four directions with the stone. Make enough space for you to move in.

This is a conscious act of arrival. This is where I am. Now.

The task is to open to each of the four directions. You can do this in a variety of different ways. You can meditate, move, or make sounds. Each stone holds the focus of each element and by being in the place of that stone physically, mentally, emotionally, you can open to the spirits of the four directions.

The kinds of questions to ask are – How do I relate to Air, Earth, Fire, and Water through my body, my thoughts, and my feelings? With which element do I have the strongest relation, and which the weakest? As a guide, Air is associated with thought processes, Fire with spirit and passion, Earth with the physical body, and Water with emotion.

When you have completed this process, go to the weakest element and ask yourself how you can develop the relation more strongly. Our aim is to balance the elements in our selves through the power of our own attention.

The Speaking wheel

My most influential teacher, Chu-Ra, talked about the elements as if they were conscious –
"The elements are playing," she would say, like everything was a wonderful work of art in progress. When the desert was still, she would say -
"The air is listening to the Sun." When the wind blew she might say –
"The air is talking to the Earth." Once there was a great windstorm and she said –
"The Earth just isn't listening!" When it rained, she said it was a good time to let go, a good time to die. Like wiping the canvas clean. Then start afresh the next day. For her the elements were real beings at play, and every turn in the weather brought out in her a secret of joy and wonder.

Chu-Ra listened so much to the wind. It talked to her. When it went in a certain direction, she would say –

"Now they are talking to the North," or – "Now they are talking to the South." And she would look in the direction of the wind like it was a sign. There may be a bird and she would follow the bird like it was leading her thoughts deeper into the Great Mystery. One day the wind was talking to the East and we watched a bird settle on a tree.

"We have to go there," she said. So we walked to the tree where the bird had landed, and we meditated. During this particular meditation I heard the four directions like they were talking to me. They were real. The tree was connecting me with Chu-Ra's intelligence. In those moments I could feel the extraordinary balancing act the dreamers perform with the four directions, the four elements, four voices. The joy. The play. Like music. What skill the dreamers had to magically transform the four vibrations into the dream of planet Earth.

Elemental thought vibrations.

In the last chapter, we looked at the idea of the universe as thought-vibrations. Dreamers design their dream by changing the speed of these thought vibrations. The speed is the time between the dreamer sees and the dreamer sees again. This makes a time circle which can be repeated. One circle of seeing may be enough to establish a dot in space for a milli-second, but it would need many circles of repeated sight to build up a sustained object in the dream.

To build something sustained in mind space requires fast repeated attention. If there is a long gap between seeing and seeing again, the object can easily be forgotten. It is like someone who tries to write a sentence and begins with one word, pauses, then forgets the sentence. Or someone who starts building a house on a Caribbean island, builds the walls, leaves it for a year, and comes back to find that all has been blown down by a hurricane. The forces against the holding of the dream in time and space are phenomenal. To hold it in place requires the sustained attention of time circles. The more the dreamer consciously sees the dream, the more firm the connection between the seer and the seen. The dense circles of time protect the illusion in a tunnel from the random chaos of pure thought.

Dreamers use many skills to make an object apparently solid. To describe this process I will need to bring in other ways of describing thought vibrations. Firstly, it could be said that the universe was sung or hummed into existence. By changing the frequency of vibration, the sound could be higher or lower in pitch. The dreamers were the first great musicians. They were like a pianist learning to play without books or teacher. Make a sound. Listen to the sound. Develop the sound by repeating with some alterations. The four elements are like a full-sustained four-note chord around which the melodies can dance.

Thought vibration is also colour. The faster the vibration, the lighter the colour; the slower the vibration, the darker the colour. Colours are sounds, sounds are colours. Subtle sounds can be painted and soft colours can be sung.

Another denominator is temperature. The fast vibration is hotter and the slower vibration colder.

The molecular design is also an important part of the magic. Each thought vibration is a dot, an atomic particle. To slow the thought down into form, the dreamer concentrates many particles together by sustaining attention. It is like a pointillist painting. Each dreaming attention creates a dot, and the object of the dream is built with each attention.

The density of thought molecules will determine the nature of the form. For example, Fire molecules will be less dense than Water molecules. Fire moves faster than Water, and so needs a lighter touch. Air is the least dense of the elements, and Earth has the most density.

The fixed attention of Earth requires more sophisticated design. The dreamers learn how to intensify the dots into lines and curves from which it is possible to develop compound shapes like circles and triangles. With these design tools, all forms are possible.

To summarise, an object is fixed through the control of perspective, sound, colour, temperature and molecular design. But there is more information. To get to the secret of the dreamers' magic, we can refer again to the law of opposites. The creative elemental cycle is clockwise.

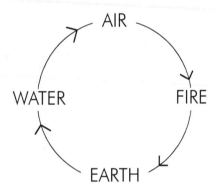

This is the time cycle between the dreamer and the dream. There is also an anti-clockwise cycle. This is the equivalent distance between the dreamer and the light source of pure thought.

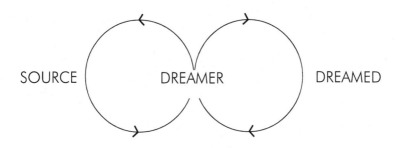

SOURCE — DREAMER — DREAMED

The anti-clockwise cycle starts with the same place — the intent to see, but rather than gripping the energy in an attempt to control, the dreamer releases the energy into the unknown. The result is not Fixed Attention, but No Attention. Enlightenment. The dreamer circles back to the source and in effect disappears into the One Mind — a speck of time into timelessness. The dreamer then intends itself through Fire to return to the dreamtime.

The nature of the anti-clockwise time cycle is much more fluid and playful. Innocent. It is the energy of dance and play. Forms come, then go. It is of no matter. Inside every solid object is this world of energy at play — dots, circles, lines, curves, shapes, sounds, colours, sensations. A powerful microscopic camera will reveal all. The whole of the apparently fixed world is vibrating.

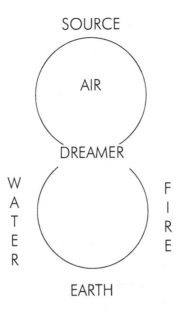

SOURCE

AIR

DREAMER

W
A
T
E
R

F
I
R
E

EARTH

The world of the anti-clockwise time circle can be accessed very easily during sleep. When the mind relaxes, the clockwise elemental fixed attention cycle is harder to maintain. The control goes and the dreamer slips into the opposite circle. The sleep is the time between the dreamer sees and sees again. If you sleep for a long time, or have a deep dream, you can wake up disorientated and wonder where you are, or even if you are! The anti-clockwise spiral releases what is held, and this can cause anxiety and stress. The anxiety is fear of letting go into the unknown. Nightmares are a painful resistance to the anti-clockwise movement. Yet the fully conscious dreamer knows the chaos inside order and the order inside chaos; the destructive within the creative and the creative within the destructive (See chapter nine). The two circles spin in unison.

The clockwise:

And the anti-clockwise.

These ancient Hindu signs can be found in both directions on ancient Balinese temples. The symbol means – the law.

The Dreamers' Elemental Magic

The laws that the dreamers learnt would hold the projection in place by itself. It is like a magician who is attending to spinning plates and then suddenly discovers a law that keeps the plates spinning by themselves. The magician doesn't have to keep running around spinning them by hand. Once the laws were in place, the hologram was transformed into a fixed state that no longer needed the constant focus of the dreamer's mind. They could focus on other things.

The architect had to learn how to make bricks. The first building I constructed at the Dreaming temple in Mexican desert, was for me a taste of this principal in action. I was dreaming a roundhouse but had no idea how to build one. In the desert, they make bricks out of sand and donkey manure

(Earth), and Water. They leave it in the sun (Fire) to dry. There are good and bad quality bricks depending on how much Air is in the mixture. If the sand is fine, and they dry quickly, the bricks stick. If the sand is brittle and they don't dry easily, the brick is more likely to crumble. The skill of the magical brick maker is in his knowledge of how the elements combine.

When the first building at the temple was made, it was a relief for it to be out of my head. It will survive by itself for many years with a little maintenance.

The human body is also a building constructed from the elements. The element of Air is in the breath, the element of Fire in the warming of the blood, the element of Earth in the bones, and the element of Water in the liquid, which makes up roughly two-thirds of our construction. The body, like a building, can be made strong or weak depending on the elemental magicians who construct it. Unlike the building, the human body needs constant maintenance, and in some cases some heavy repair work to maintain or develop the elemental balance. The reason for this is that the human body is much more sophisticated than an adobe building, and needs a lot more energy to maintain it in fixed attention.

Matter is still projection of mind, a thought-vibration, but it is a fixed thought projection, which follows certain laws. The medicine wheel teaches us how to follow the laws of our body and find balance in our lives.

Exercise 6. The Portable Medicine Wheel

The human body is composed of the four elements so it is very easy for us to relate to them consciously all the time. We can give ourselves a basic balance check as we go.

The element of Air we relate to with every breath. We need

oxygen in our bodies to survive. Most of us do not breathe deeply enough and so we deny ourselves the oxygen we need. The signs of lack of oxygen are sluggishness and lack of energy. There is even a very expensive oxygen therapy available in fashionable Harley Street using very sophisticated equipment to pump the starving body with what it could naturally intake - just by breathing. Deeply. Deep breaths can be taken anywhere. They are free. Air is free. It gives us energy. Take what you need at no extra cost!

People with too much Air tend to feel hot. Also hot-headed! Hyperventilation will effect those who do too much too quickly, either with the body or the intellect. In this case slow down and breathe gently.

Fire in the body is from the heart. The heart is our internal engine and it feeds from Air. They're all in it together. The breath can regulate the body temperature. Tibetan Buddhists develop fast and slow breathing exercises to regulate the temperature of the body even in the high Himalayas. Fast breathing will raise the temperature of the body; slow breathing will cool it down. We can also get a lot of help from the Sun, which is also free but not always available. In countries like England, particularly in winter, it is a case of taking the opportunity when it arises. The Sun is the purest form of fire and in an English winter a pure gift from the heavens! Apart from the Sun, movement and exercise will keep the heart healthy. Visualising the Sun, or the colours red and orange, can also bring internal heat. If there is too much heat, the body needs to slow down, and the colour blue will help. Regulating the breath and colour visualisations are very handy portable ways of controlling body temperature. When the temperature of the body is well tuned, like a car, it will run smoothly.

The amount of Earth in your body will determine how strong

is your structure and also how heavy and light you are. Bones and limbs need feeding, so maintaining a good diet is important for a strong body. If your Earth element is weak, you are more likely to float off, and it is difficult to concentrate and achieve things on this planet. In this case, focus on your diet and exercises so that you become more focused on your physical body. Meditative movements like yoga and Chi Kong are particularly helpful. If your Earth element is too strong, you are likely to feel heavy and stuck. A lot of Air and Fire is needed. Deep breathing and more physically demanding exercise will help. Also a daring adventure in the sun! Time to get up and move.

The element of Water constitutes two thirds of our body and like Air we tend not to get enough of it. When natural water flows through our system, it cleans us. If the body feels sluggish, a fast of drinking only water, even for a day, can revitalise the engine. Make sure the water is natural and not treated. Too much water can affect bodies with low metabolism.

The medicine wheel is our internal doctor and we don't need to make appointments. The key again is listening. Depth of breath, body temperature, heaviness or lightness, clean or sluggish engine. It's your body.

The Human Dreamers who Dream us

The medicine wheel presents a way of becoming aware of the most powerful human dreamers in our lives. Consider the following medicine wheel.

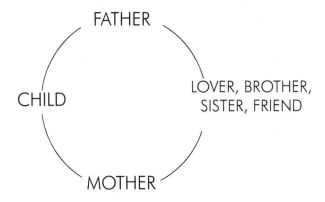

FATHER

CHILD

LOVER, BROTHER, SISTER, FRIEND

MOTHER

The union between the father and the mother is the place of the creative fire. It can be seen as the wish to continue their dream. This is a very powerful dream projection. The father and the mother have many needs and wishes for the baby. Not only is there the wish to continue the dream, but also projected onto the baby is the unfulfilled needs of the parents – the needs of the lover, the brother, the sister, the friend. These needs and wishes will also be informed by the cultural dream, the dream of the country in which the baby is born. The strength of the dream of the mother, the dream of the father, the dream of the culture is very intense. The child will be very strongly influenced by these dreams and they control the child into adult life.

The way in which someone or something dreams us, is the way in which someone 'sees' us. The mother, for example, projects onto the child an image of who the child is. The dream in her mind is so strong; the child becomes, to some extent, the image of how the mother sees him/her.

By connecting with the basic elements of how we are being dreamed, we can feel the roots of our habits, our actions, and our inactions. When we touch the root of our behaviour, we have, at least, the opportunity to change. Furthermore, by aligning ones energy with the primal elemental principles, one becomes not only a co-creator of ones developing personality, but also the co-creator of the developing dream of the Earth.

Exercise 7. **Meeting the Human Dreamer.**

This medicine wheel represents the main influences of human dreamers in our lives. The following exercise is to help develop an awareness of how these dreams influence us.

Go to the place of the North. How has and does the relationship with your father, either your father by blood or your adopted father, influence your life? In what way are you doing what he wants? In what ways are you in reaction to what he wants? What are the cultural dreams – the dreams of the nation, the dreams of his period in history – which influenced your father? How do those cultural dreams influence your life?

Go to the place of the South. Consider your relationship with your mother. Ask yourself the same questions as you did for your father.

Go to the place of the East. See if you can feel the lover, friend, brother, sister, that your parents were trying (consciously or unconsciously) to dream through you.

Go to the place of the west, the child. How have you been dreamed? Can you feel any other dreams that influenced your child besides your mother, your father and your culture?

At least when we are conscious of how we are being dreamed, we begin to have some choice over how the dream continues.

These exercises to understand the relationship between the dreamer and the dreamed are developed gradually as the book progresses.

FOUR: ROCKS

In order to develop further, the dreamers had to do something they hadn't done before. Up to this point they had treated the universe like their own laboratory, and they always had a certain distance in their attitude. They were essentially observers of phenomenon, but they could see that this separation of observer and observed, was something of a limitation. They realised that in order to go further they had to invest a part of themselves in what they were creating. To some extent, they had to become what they were designing. In some of their more developed creations, they planted a seed of their own consciousness. This seed was made of crystal.

The dreamers chose crystal to hold the seed of their consciousness because it was of form and not of form at the same time. They had designed crystal to grow into a very strong structure. Yet despite its strength of focus into form, it could hold all the hologramatic thoughts of the dreamers' early days. It could hold the traces of the connections between dreams right back to the first impulse to design. In short, crystal had the capacity to store the complete history of the dream from the first breath. Moreover, it could continue to store all the development of the dream from the seed of the designer's consciousness.

What the dreamers did was to risk part of themselves in their own creation. They planted seeds of themselves in every planet in which they had a particular interest without giving themselves entirely away. They made themselves into the subject as well as the object; the observed as well as the observer; the experiment as well as the experimenters. They were completely involved in a way they had never been before.

From the perspective of the planets, this injection of the seed into their centre was like the Gods coming to land. In terms of planet Earth mythology it was like an alien invasion. It was alien because the Earth had never been touched before by the hand of its creator. It had only really been a material thought projection of a developed idea. But the dreamers wanted to touch what they had made. They wanted to experience what it is like to be made of the elements. From now on, the dreamers would have to experience everything that they conceived. So they began to take more care.

My father, a Roman Catholic, used to express sadness when he looked at what he called 'nature'. He said it was like he was looking at television. He could never be a part of it. This always saddened me. The problem is in that infamous phrase in the book of Genesis – "Man has dominion over creation." It is this, for me, which sets up the separation, the alienation from the outside. The more I explored the shamanic path, the more alive 'creation' became. Going for a walk, looking at a rock, sitting on a rock, is like interacting with an old friend who has been around a lot longer than me. The form is different, but the root is the same. The breath is the same.

Most Christians tend to believe that only humans have soul, only humans have consciousness. For them, a rock is something dead. Unconscious. All my shamanic teachers on the contrary have a consciousness of the whole world being alive. EVERYTHING HAS SOUL. Rocks are part of the soul of the universal dream. This is a huge jump to make. Everything vibrates with the energy of the universal breath.

It took me some time to understand how fundamental this difference is. I think I finally got the hang of it in Bolivia. I was studying with various curanderos (shamanic healers) in the Andes village of Charazani. I had been travelling for some months, walking with a donkey who (not always kindly) carried my pack. As I walked, I noticed how constant was my internal dialogue. When I arrived at this mountain village, I became so aware of how my internal dialogue gets in the way of everything else.

There is a beautiful river near the village and I used to go and sit on a particular rock. I would listen to my internal dialogue for hours. It felt like I was trying to hold onto something. There was a fear of what would happen if I didn't hear a human voice – any human voice. So many people I know will turn on the television or radio and listen to anything rather than be in silence. Here I was carrying my own television and radio inside my head. I realised I had never really arrived at Charazani, or anywhere in Bolivia, or any other country. I was travelling in my own television set, and it didn't matter where I was, it was pretty much the same soap opera. One day, in exasperation, I said to the rock –

"How do I switch it off?"

The rock acted like it was waiting for me to realise it existed. The 'act' of the rock was to move my body into a position where I could hear it. The energy of the rock extends into air and could move my body if I was open to receiving its vibration. The television was preventing me from receiving the frequency of the rock. When I opened to the rock, there was the beginning of an interaction. The rock could both give and receive energy. Its thoughts moved my body into a position where my internal dialogue was flooded with sounds. These sounds were the sounds of the rock, the sounds of the land, the mountains. Their huge voices drowned out my internal dialogue and transformed my experience.

The body merged into the sounds and it began to move as if it was being sung. I felt I was hearing the Earth body; I was being moved by the Earth body. The Earth body was moving through me. It was communicating through me.

My human body extended from the Earth body and reached out. The Moon, Mars, Venus, the solar system, the universe. The rock was showing me how the universe is a body, and each bone in the universal body relates to the human skeleton. The rock bones of planet Earth relate to the rock bones of Mars, the Moon, Pluto, and planets outside the solar system. All the planetary bones interconnect the universal body. I could feel them, hear them through my own sensations. On this rock I was moving my human body, Earth body, Universal body.

Rocks reflect the bones of the universe

No planet was made in isolation. The elemental experiments took place all over the universe. The rocks are both the bones and the memory of the initial elemental experiments. They hold thought matter in time and place. The Earth planetary rock relates to the rock formations on other planets. They come from the same dream, the same design intention. By listening to rocks, it is not only possible to read the history of this planet Earth; it is also possible to read the related history of other planets in the universe.

The universe is a body. It is a body of thought. It is a body made by mind. The bones of the universal body all relate like the bones of a human skeleton. The rock bones of planet Earth relate to the rock bones of Mars, the Moon, Pluto and planets outside our solar system. All the planetary bones interconnect the universal body, and each planetary bone structure is the base of a particular function in the universal body.

Rocks are part of the soul of the universal dream. In the dream of the universe, EVERYTHING HAS SOUL. The soul is the essence of something. The essence of the universe is breath, and breath comes from nothing. This is not the nothing of negation; this is the nothing of everything. The All of Nothing. Completion. You and I are made of the same essence as rock. We all share the same soul. We are all breathed into the universal dream. A rock is part of the universal breath.

Listening to the Stone People

All stones and rocks are useful, and any stone can teach us something. You can find a stone to work with on the beach, in a field, on a hill, in your garden, on the road. It is a great exercise to go to a stony place like a beach and feel which ones you are attracted to. It is amazing to discover that of all the thousands of stones on the beach, there are one or two which just feel right. There may not appear be a particular reason. They are just right for you. It can change the beach experience for life when you lay down on the stones and realise that each one is vibrating, living, breathing with the universe!

The stone is your precious philosopher. It holds the secrets of the creation of this planet and other planets in the universe. To access the information requires the developed Art of Listening. The Art to Listening is to find a space where there isn't much distraction. Distraction inside and distraction outside. A breath awareness meditation is the perfect preparation. Then open your mind to the reality that the stone is alive and has information for you. Meditate with it. Move with it. The stone is like a guide and will lead you. The information may not be expressed in words, it may be expressed through your movement, colour, or through touch. You may feel to massage a particular area of your body to which the stone is taking your attention. Some stones speak through rhythm. Beach stones can make great percussion. If the stone is small, it is a good idea to sleep with it under the pillow. Stones speak a lot through the night dreams.

The North American tribes call them the Stone People. The more you open your mind and your senses to the stones, the more they will speak to you.

Exercise 8. **Stones and the Chakras**

Different stones have particular vibration frequencies, which relate to our chakras. Chakras are energy points on the human body. They are the means through which the human body relates to all other beings on this planet and all other life in the universe.

There are various systems of chakras, which range from 4 to 38. The most widely used system is with seven. The following exercise will help you to feel where your chakras are as well as develop your relationship with the Stone People.

First of all buy or find seven stones of different colours and type. Take your time discovering them.

Take your attention to the base chakra. The base chakra is between the scrotum and anus for men and between the vagina and anus for women. Connect the stone you feel is right for this chakra. Meditate on this chakra. Visualise the colour of the stone in the area of the chakra. Take the stone itself to the chakra area. The chakra points have a specific focus on the body, which is subtly different for each person. You are trying to feel where the chakra is on your body.

What does this chakra relate to for you?

What kinds of thoughts and feelings does it bring up in you?

Allow yourself to explore your relation with your own base chakra.

Take your attention to the second chakra. This is above the

groin and below the navel. Which stone relates to this chakra? Repeat the same process as with the base chakra.

Repeat the exercise for the other five chakras:

Chakra three is in the solar plexus area beneath the ribs and above the navel.

Chakra four is the heart chakra in the chest area.

Chakra five is the throat chakra.

Chakra six is the third eye chakra on the temple of the head.

Chakra seven is the crown chakra at the top of the head.

When you have finished the exercise, focus your attention for at least five minutes on your feet and their relation with the Earth.

There is more chakra work later, and it will be interesting to see if the relations you find for yourself are similar to their description in chapter 8.

Journey to the Centre of the Earth

A very strong experience with rocks for me was in Mexico. I had been walking with a shaman in the north who encouraged me to pay more attention to the messages that come through the medium of rocks, so my sense of hearing rock energy had been finely attuned. I was travelling from the desert down the pacific coast, and camped out one night on the beach. Apart from the roar of the great pacific waves, my mind was alive with a sense of someone trying to talk to me. I could hear very faint messages. The moon was strong, almost full, and the sky was so clear, the stars were touching me. I experienced a sense of being touched by the light from the stars. I could feel the planet Earth like it was huddled in a group of friends, and their communication was through the energy of light.

I sat under a cliff, my back against a rock. I could feel my body sinking into the sand, and my attention was taken deeper into the rock in the cliff. With every breath, my attention was taken deeper. I could feel myself being drawn through red tunnels. The journey was taking me into the planet, breath after breath, and through all the red, a sense of liquid, of underground rivers. I was being taken down into the planet like I was floating with my breath through deep rivers, and yet still I could feel the rock through my back vibrating as if it was alive, pulsing into my bones. I was trying to breathe in unison with the pulsing of the rock, and the slow vibration was taking me deeper through the rivers of energy. I began to feel the tunnels of energy opening out, and colours leading away like root fibres.

I began to see forms, strange forms of colour and light that were travelling with me. We were all on a journey, a long long journey, and some I passed because they were slower than I was, and some faster beings passed me. We all had a different pace and a different form, yet we were all going in the same direction. Soon the forms became clearer, and I could make out humans, animals, composite creatures like centaurs and griffins, and some creatures I had never seen before. Still I could feel the vibration of the rock, and I felt like I was being breathed by the rock. The rock set the pace of my breath and so the pace of my journey deeper into the planet.

I floated with my breath through the underground rivers, and the forms of the great procession crystallised into a scene so real, I could feel the whole of my body in this dream. I was travelling over a large plain with the dinosaurs that had been walking this path ever since their demise thousands of years ago. The land was wide and long, and the dinosaurs heavy and weary. I felt very light by comparison and could glide past them like a bird. It felt like we were all being drawn towards the same place. We were all on the same journey. Bird and beast and man.

My dream moved on with my breath. My body felt it could do things that I couldn't do in the physical body. I could breathe through the rivers that moved me, I could see through the surface of the scenes that presented themselves, I could fly, I could merge with the other energy around me. Everything was alive as if there was no difference between the energy I was perceiving and the energy of my body. My dreaming body. My body was being dreamed to the centre of the planet. With every breath, the rock was breathing me deeper into the Earth dream.

I met so many other creatures on their way, some of them walking, some of them crawling, some of them swimming, some of them flying. A black beetle. An ant. A woman. A fish. A green cloudy being, a red pointed being, a blue mist, spots of purple. Energy. Different forms of energy making their way to the centre. And I began to hear sounds, very faint whispering sounds. I felt my ears being kissed, and I had a sense of the stars touching me through the sound and breathing me through the rock. The light was finding its way through my dreaming to the centre.

I could feel the ends of the breath and had the feeling I was nearing my destination. There, at the edge of this dream, four gold Buddhas were sitting around a white globe. The globe was like water, and fire. Fire in water. The four Buddhas were sitting, waiting, receiving. All the forms of energy journey towards the centre and here the four Gold Buddhas received them. They were the great guardians of the white globe, which was our destination. We had all been breathed into the white crystal centre of the planet. I had been shown the journey of the soul. Here in the middle of the four Golden Buddhas was the great crystal centre of true death, of pure transformation.

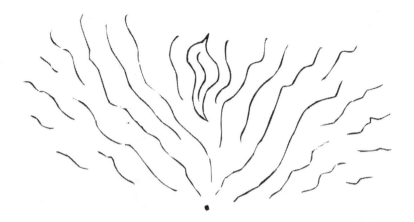

Quartz Crystal

Some years after this journey, I understood how it described the elemental journey of the soul. This is described in more detail in Chapter nine. It also described the importance of crystal. Quartz crystal came after the rocks formed by the original elemental experiments. It is different from other rocks because it grows. It is more like a rock plant, literally.

Each rock has a different thought vibration. Quartz crystal has the fastest vibration. It is not found in general on the surface of the Earth. You have to dig for it. There is crystal throughout the planet. This crystal grid links the consciousness of the different parts of the globe. It is like the deepest part of the consciousness in the planet and so it holds the deepest secrets. The rocks on the surface are of a slower vibration and so for us easier to access. The surface rocks are like the front of the brain. They are what can be seen.

Quartz crystal is available because people have dug mountains and jungle to get at it. It is like entering the head and pulling out what has been at the back of the mind for centuries. The information should be handled with great care.

When the dreamers invested themselves in their own

ſ∪ⅠⅠ—∫—Ⅰᛰ—Ⅰ—)(⊙—Ⅰſ∪Ⅰᛰ—ⅠⅠᛰ—Ⅰ⊖—Ⅰᛰ—Ⅰⵔ

dream, things started to get serious. What had begun as play was developing into something precious – something worth living for and something worth dying for. The concept of death was somewhat irrelevant up to this point. Ideas come, ideas go with little consequence, but when ideas become action, when the dreamer becomes the dream, then things get serious. If I not only dream crystal, but become crystal also, then I have to live the consequences of being crystal.

What would it be like being crystal?

Powerful. Very very powerful. The dreamers managed to pack the essence of the first breath into the crystalline structure. This meant and means that crystal holds the force and energy of that creative hurricane. This is not some fluffy new age fantasy. This is serious power. Power that can destroy; power that can create. Quartz crystal is the power behind the modern technological revolution. There is quartz crystal at the heart of every bank, business, government organisation, school and hospital. The tiniest crystal can hold a phenomenal potential. Crystal amplifies energy. The dreamers took the force of the original breath and found for themselves a form in which they could be held. They became held in crystal.

The word `holding' is crucial. When the dreamers became, in part, of form, they took a big risk. They gave themselves to an elemental process they did not entirely understand. Technically, anything could happen. The form could disappear, and with it, the energy of themselves they had invested. The infinite energy of the first breath became finite. The energy could be lost. Power was invested with a hugely increased commitment to the project. The play in the game was over. Here was the beginning of the awareness of mortality. Now the game was about life and death.

The dreamers fell in love with themselves. The creators fell in love with their creation in a way that would cause pain if the relation should end. They became attached to their own image. They became precious about themselves. Very precious. The painters had passed their preliminary examinations and now they wanted to make something more professional. Planets like Earth were great opportunities for the aspiring artists.

The soul of the universe becomes more complicated. The dreamers would move further and further away from the original breath. They would become more deeply immersed in the separated forms, which would cause them, at times, to forget the lightness of the play. They would endeavour to prolong the work of art for as long as possible. The soul of the universe is expressed and developed into so many different forms. Yet the essence of the soul is always the same. Breath. Nothing. The beauty of completion. From the breath is the dance of the dream, and then the return. No matter how far the dreamers travel into their own dream, crystal would always hold the key of the return to the source.

Exercise 9. **The Conscious Co-creative Dreamer**

The technical effect of the planting of crystal was to create another light source. The dreamer could direct energy from inside the dream as well as from outside the dream. Not only is an object seen, but also an object 'sees'.

If we connect with our internal light, we become the dreamer as well as the dreamed. This is the part of us that can become the co-creator.

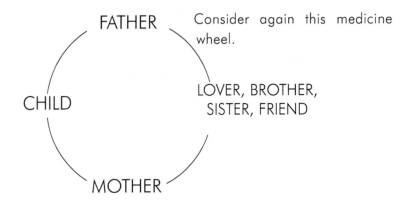

FATHER

Consider again this medicine wheel.

LOVER, BROTHER, SISTER, FRIEND

CHILD

MOTHER

Return to the place of your father. Meditate on your own father. Then expand the dream of 'father'. What does 'father' mean? What is the energy, the essence of this dream or 'father'? The crystal inside you gives you the power to project your own sense of father. You can then go to the South, and project your own sense of mother. In the east, you can project your own sense of lover, friend, brother, sister. In the west you can project your own sense of child onto yourself. The dreams expand beyond how they have appeared to you in your day to day life. The father you have known is a starting point of a much more powerful essential dream in the universe. The Mother, the Father, the Lover in the universe. They can appear in many forms. You can access the energy of these dreams by consciously re-dreaming yourself through sustained attention. Seeing. Seeing again.

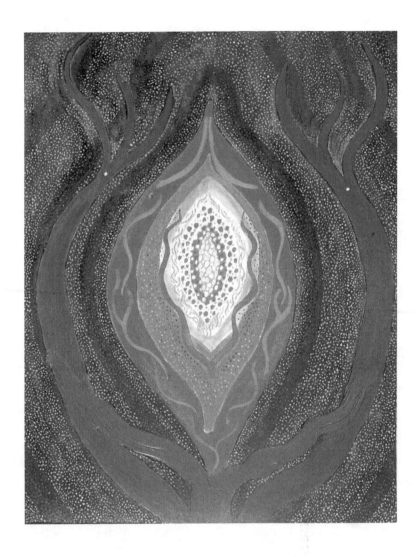

FIVE - TREES

The first masterstroke of the crystalline designer seeds was the discovery of the principle elemental construction: DNA. With this principle, itself a seed, the dreamers in the planets could extend themselves into various forms whilst the larger part of the dreamer's consciousness could observe the results. The observer could feed the results of its discoveries to the developing dream of the crystalline seed. In this way, they had the joint perspectives of inside and outside.

The first extensions of the crystal seed were understandably tentative: Simple plants, grasses, microbes, amoebas. But gradually the extensions became more daring – trees.

The dream of the tree
Is the dream of the breath
Wash of water
Earth to light
Transmitters of energy
Sky to earth
Clearing the mind of
What is no matter
Clearing the souls
That hide in the shadows
Playing with forms
In the half light

Making memories
Laugh light
Light-er –
Releasing the pain into
No matter
Playing the friend
Playing boy
Playing girl
Swing or hang or
Jump or dare
Breathing air
Like there is no matter
Making light of the dark.

Dream of the tree on the Earth
Is the lung
Dream of the tree on the Earth
Is the breath
Dream of the tree on the Earth
Is the life –
Gateway to hell
Gateway to heaven
Lower, middle and upper worlds
Bridge for the soul's
Journey to star.

Dream of the tree
Dream of the spirit
Holding the love
Deep in the woods
Fuel for the fire
Fuel for the food
Fuel for the warmth of the sleep into
Dream

Dream of the tree
Holding an answer.

Hold the bird
Hold the monkey
Hold the squirrel
Hold the snake

Feed the giraffe
Feed the elephant
Feed the monkey
Feed the man

Dream of the tree is
Light into matter -
Web into world –
Energised form
Vibrating at all the
Universal rates
Translating daily in
Languages unheard.

Dream of the tree
Opens the heart,
Reveals the
Song of the Earth.

I am grateful to trees for helping me heal. I was very ill in London, before I consciously started on this path, and was sleeping about fifteen hours each night. When I was awake, I could not concentrate or do anything. No energy. My defences were down and all the noise and ugliness of the city entered into my body. I developed a deep anger of the human race! This illness lasted a long time, and the doctors had no answers. The only relief I found was when I went to a park and sat under a tree. It was always the same tree, an oak. When I sat underneath it, I felt less angry and at times even at peace. After a while, I wondered why I always went to the same tree, and I visited other trees. I discovered how different each tree is. They all have their own quality, like people. I used to call my daily visits 'tree therapy' because I would talk to them and ask them questions. They would always come up with an answer, usually in the form of taking my attention to a particular plant, or a particular butterfly, a bird, a cloud. This gave me a new perspective and so I found fresh ideas, sounds, feelings. The answers would come in their own way, and their would always be a sense of relief. Trees are very wise, and it was their counselling which helped me recover.

Many years later in Darwin, Australia, I developed a friendship with an Aboriginal man called Tony. Like many Aboriginals, when he was a young child, he was taken away from his family and 'adopted' into a white middle class home. He rebelled and sought to find the roots of his culture. He travelled to visit the elders of his tribe to learn from them.

When we met, we always sat under a tree. This was their way. A meeting always took place under a tree, not only for the shade, he told me, but so that the tree can also listen and advise. He explained to me how the energy of trees moves, and his ideas linked with what I had learned in Mexico and Nepal.

Trees reflect the lungs of the universe

It is not only water that the tree brings up through its roots. Its censors can pick up signals as far down as the centre of the Earth. The tree brings the energy of the crystalline core of the Earth to the surface of the planet through its extra-sensory filaments in the roots. The energy pulses through the tree in union with the tree's continuous transformative breath – oxygen to carbon dioxide. The filaments on the leaves have the same extra sensory perception as the filaments on the roots. They connect to the universal web of energy, which connects this planet with other planets and other star systems. Trees are constantly transmitting energy from Earth to star and star to Earth. They are the telephone exchange systems between Earth and all other galaxies in the universe.

Imagine what it would be like if you could draw a diagram of all your thoughts; how they criss-cross, zigzag, go straight and then curve or tie themselves in knots.

The universe is also a mind of thought shapes. Some organised, some disorganised, but all in some way connected. They are all dreamed. They are dream lines. Your mind is a microcosm of the universe. The lines in your mind, like the universe, all have a sound vibration, a different sound. They are song lines. The connections between thoughts are dreamed by waves of energy. Dreamwaves.

You can draw your mind, you can sing your mind, and you can move your mind. You can draw the universe, you can sing the universe, and you can move the universe.

A planet is a dense concentration of thought patterns. Each planet has been dreamed in a different way, but the stuff of the dream is always the same: thought-vibration. The concentrations of thoughts, which make up a planet, are connected to other planets' thought concentrations through

Air Space. Air Space is less concentrated, less dense. Yet even though Air Space does not contain material thought, there are non-material thoughts, invisible. The strongest of these non-material thoughts is like a trunk road that links one planet with another. This is often called the Cosmic Web spun by the dreamweaver: the spider.

The cosmic spider is a phenomenal invention. It continually cleans the Cosmic Web by consuming thought concentrates that get stuck. Thoughts get caught in circles like habits. They can't move on. They repeat themselves, and this blocks the passage of information through the Cosmic Web.

The human body is no different than the universal body. There is a web which connects the various energetic centres in our bodies, and if this web is blocked, the human body, like the universal body cannot receive the energetic information it needs to function. In the human body, the thoughts that get stuck are like the babbling of madmen or the constantly repeated themes of a soap opera. They are spirits, energetic beings that possess the body and hold it in their circle because they don't know where else to go and are frightened of taking the risk of the unknown. The cosmic spider of the human body saves the possessive spirit from its own hell. The repeated soap opera loses its appeal, and there is space for more information to enter.

The word 'information' can mean many things: words, sounds, colours, feelings or sensations. There are many languages in the dream.

No planet was dreamed in isolation. The dreamers experimented with many spaces and the information learnt from one planetary experience was fed into other planetary experiences. Trees were and are the means through which the experience was and is shared. With each breath they are communicating the information of the Earth planetary experience to similar devices on other planets and stars.

It is through trees that the dreamers could effectively

function inside and outside their creation at the same time. The trees feed information to other parts of the universal mind-body, which gives the dreamers a clearer perspective. They can be subject and object; the dreamer and the dreamed; seeing and seen.

If rocks are the windows to other planetary dreams then trees are the messengers. The messages are sent and received with each breath. This information is vital for the health of this planet. Through this information, the planet maintains its perspective in the universal body. The information is like blood. If blood does not reach the stomach, for example, the stomach cannot function. Trees pump blood into the planetary body and the planetary body would die without them.

The heart of our solar system is the Sun, the star. The star is the generator of energy. Trees and plants know how to transform the solar energy and feed it into the planet. The Sun that we see is connected to all the other stars in the universe. The trees bring stellar information through the Sun to this planet. They know how to digest it and make it useful.

This is crucial for the health of both you and me. The human body is interconnected with the Earth planetary body. We need the information of other stars and planets for our balance and healing. The cosmic spider can only do so much. Right now, the song lines are blocked and it takes a great effort to listen. It is more difficult to be fluid and to act from the place of no doubt. Not only do we need trees for our health; we need to learn how to receive the information that they bring and how to give through them what we know. The word 'information,' I repeat, can come in many forms. The stars touch us in many ways, and it is often as simple as feeling better.

Exercise 10. **Tree Healing**

The healing of a tree works by breaking the pattern of a circle. The tree is bringing in new information, which is a breath of fresh air. The tree gives a break from the internal dialogue; the continuous mad chattering of the preoccupied mind which also damages the physical body. The tree cleans the mind and opens it to new possibilities.

To heal through a tree is very easy. Spend time with them. It is like medicine. Five minutes a day. Ten minutes. Fifteen minutes. The time it takes to co-ordinate the human breath with the breath of the tree. This is possible if you open your energy body to the tree like you would open your energy bodies to a lover. Open to giving energy with your out-breath and receiving energy with your in-breath. The tree does not think intellectually, it does not need to think. It is living entirely on continuous impulse; it is already an enlightened being.

When the human physical body is ill, it has lost harmony with its environment. The energy of the human body is part of an intricate web of energies linking human to planet and planet to planet. The breath of a tree is in touch with the co-ordination of the WHOLE movement. It is a symphony. Just sit, relax, and press play.

The body will find its own way home.
The body knows how to heal itself.

The body is already connected to the source of all energy.

The tree helps the body to remember.

After a while of sitting and breathing, begin to move. You don't have to think. Move under a tree. The body knows where it wants to go, what to move, how. Finger, thumb, arm, foot. No need to think. The body knows everything without thinking.

SIX - ANIMAL GUIDES

*Gradually the extensions became more daring –
trees, insects, fish, and eventually reptiles and
mammals.*

Animals reflect the limbs of the universe

Walking at night in the Australian bush with Tony, my Aboriginal friend, the stars feel so close, you can touch them – "That's where the kangaroo people go," he says, pointing to a beautiful pattern of white in the sky.

"And there is where the crocodile people go."

The night sky becomes a description of the animal dreaming. The Earth and the stars are part of the same dream and the aboriginal moves effortlessly from one part of the dream to the other. The Earth and the stars in the sky are part of the same universal body. The animals describe the parts of the body. As above, so below. The animals on Earth are the animals in the heavens.

In Guatemala, I came across another aspect of the same idea. Every animal has a star. In fact it is the star which dreams them. The animal does not exist in the star like it does here in its material form, since no animal could live somewhere like the sun! However, their spirit lives there. Their essence or soul lives in the star and it is from there that they derive their power.

The animals in the stars are parts of the universal body. Each animal has a specific function in the universal body. Animals have no doubt as to their meaning and purpose like an arm or a leg has no doubt as to what their relation is with the rest of the body. The arm works in co-ordination with the shoulder, the hand, and the rest of the body. The animal functions like a universal limb and has no doubt as to what its function is. Unlike humans, they do not need to question themselves.

Animals have interconnecting relations with other animals in the universal body. Hunger is the strongest form of their communication on Earth. When the eagle eats the mouse, the eagle links the eagle star dream to the mouse star dream. This intensifies the link like the strengthening of a muscle in that part of the universal body. The mouse is an extraordinary being because it is also linked to the snake. The snake also eats the mouse. The star of the mouse is linked to the star of the snake and the star of the eagle. The interconnections in the food chain reflect the interconnections between different stars in the universal body.

In Mexican mythology, the relationship between the eagle and the snake is particularly significant. The Aztec City of Mexico is built where it is because the elders were told in their dreaming that they should look for the place where the eagle is standing on a cactus, eating a snake. This image is seen all over Mexico, even on the coins. The snake is the symbol of the Earth, the eagle a symbol of the sky (the heavens). The eagle takes the energy of the snake, through eating it. The snake eagle flies into the heavens. The Earth dances into the sky. It is a symbol of ascendancy.

Animals are guides in the non-material dream. This is generally understood by all of my shamanic teachers. During vision quests, animals can show us how to journey deeper into ourselves. In Mexico, the tribes of the Northwest walk for three months to arrive at a sacred mountain. This sacred trek is called the Huricuta, and the people come in search of a vision of the deer. The deer is a revered symbol and will show them what is their purpose in this life.

The Dreaming Body

Animals are teachers of the non-material dream because they can move with fluidity from the third to the fourth dimension. Our dreaming body can take us into non-material spaces which feel, and in reality are, as real as the material. The dreaming body is the part of us which travels through vision at night, or in the conscious and unconscious dreaming of the day. The dreaming body lifts off the physical body. It travels, at times very fast, into spaces the physical body cannot enter. A very skilful conscious dreamer can be aware of being in many places at once, bridging the gaps between different parts of the Earth dream, and even the universal dream.

The dreaming body does not follow the same rules as the physical body. It can do things the physical body cannot do. The dreaming body can fly. It can swim and breathe underwater, or burrow into the Earth. In the fourth dimension, the Earth dream opens into a reality that is much more fluid, like a surreal film which changes speeds. In this dimension, everything has a form, but the forms can change. They can shape-shift. Animals have an instinctive understanding of this dimension of the dream. They can move very easily between the two dimensions, and so they can teach us. They can teach the dreaming body how to fly like a bird, how to swim like a fish, how to burrow like a badger. Through animal guides, the dreaming body learns to be versatile beyond the experience of the physical body.

I am very often dreamed into the ocean. I am dreamed deep down into the water and I have had to seek the help of the whale to learn the secrets of the ocean depths. To do this I have to bow, as it were, to the spirit of the whale, and ask it to be my teacher. It shows me how to transform the vibration of my dreaming body so that it is like a whale, and if I give myself entirely to the energy of the animal, I experience wholeness. The main technique is with the breath, which connects the physical body with the dreaming body. The control of the texture of the breath co-ordinated with the inner vision, can create that sense of the body being in two places at once.

Exercise 11. **Conscious Dreaming**
Meeting Your Animal Guide

A Conscious Dreaming session is, as it suggests, a focused time in which we become conscious of the dream. Animals are guides in the dream of our lives. They can help us to understand some of the different spaces we move into as our awareness expands. To connect with your animal guide, a rhythmic instrument like a drum will be needed. A rattle or simply two sticks can also work.

A Conscious Dreaming session is like a ceremony. It begins with smudging. Smudging is a way of cleaning a space. Smudge sticks are made of various herbs. You can make them yourself with the herbs you like to burn or you can buy them in a healing shop. The smudge makes a smoke like incense and it should be taken around the whole of your space. Set up your altar, lighting your candle, and from the candle, light the smudge. Start with the perimeters in a clockwise direction and then spiral towards the centre. As you are smudging, intend with your mind, the action of clearing and cleaning away any confused energy, which could block your vision. You could sing or hum your intention, or make a simple prayer like:

MAY THIS SPACE BE CLEAR!

Fine. A breath awareness meditation for about ten minutes will gradually open the mind. Then make your intention clear to both yourself and to the universe that you wish to meet an animal guide.

Begin to drum. The pace is up to you. You could sing to your guide, this will help. The drum will take you on a journey. You may pass through various images. An animal may appear fleetingly or will linger. Your attitude to the animal should be of a pupil to a teacher. Humility is a huge key in this exercise. This is your guide. Ask the animal to show you why it has appeared to you. The answer may be in words; it may be in feelings, sensations, or images. The animal may take you on a journey. Follow. The landscape of this conscious dream will teach you. If you can, look into the guide's eyes. The animal may change form (shape-shift), in which case go with whatever is presented. When you feel the session is over, thank the guide. Return to the breath awareness for five minutes.

You can return to the guide in subsequent sessions. This will deepen your relationship with your guide. It is very unlikely you will get all the information in one go. My relationships with animal guides are a lifetime's learning.

If you don't meet an animal guide the first time, don't give up. If your heart is open and your intent is clear, your time will come.

I learnt a very useful way of connecting with animal guides through movement with Surprapto Suryodarmo in Indonesia. The exercise starts from the place of stillness. Breathing. The intention is made to connect with the animal guides. The eyes are closed. Waiting. The body begins to move on its own accord, without any instruction or direction; it just begins to move, as if by magic. It is like a clay model that suddenly has an animator. The body moves. No reason, no control. If it is given the space, the body finds its own sense of where it wants to go. The effect on the inner vision, on what is seen inside and what is felt and sensed, is extraordinary. Animals begin to come through the body. The spirits of animals move the human body and take the human through the dream by moving the limbs. The human body becomes a channel of animal guides.

This was an exercise in opening up to the experience of being dreamed. The dreaming journeys usually ended with a sense of meeting something beautiful. A glimpse of the dreamer who dreams us. It was a feeling, a sense of joining with a truth, of falling in love. The animals help us on our journey to that deep profound sense of home.

Healing With Animal Guides

Often when we are attracted to an animal, out attention is being taken to a particular part of the universal body. Likewise it is our journey to attend to a particular part of our physical body. The physical body 'contains' the universal body. Each part of our physical body is connected to a part of the earth body, and each part of the earth body is connected to the universal body. The healing of one is the healing of all.

When we connect to a particular animal, we connect with a particular part of our human body. During a conscious dreaming session, you can request that the animal show you the part of the body to which it relates. If your relation to the animal is clear, it will show you how to relate to that part of your body. For example, you may be guided to move your body in a particular way, or to eat or drink something to feed it what it needs. Also, the energy that is held in that part of the body may need to move to another part of the body. The animal will show you how to do this. You can always ask if you are not sure. Sometimes different animals link up different parts of the body. Sometimes parts of the body relate to more than one animal – the language of interconnection has been developing for centuries.

A personal example. My spine was stiff and aching so I sang for assistance. A crocodile came and moved my body to lay on my stomach. I began to move like a crocodile, particularly making curved movements of my spine. The whole body made shapes like waxing and waning moons. I had the crocodile in my vision the whole time and felt an extraordinary movement of energy through the whole of my body. Eventually it came to rest, and then I saw a giraffe. I stood up and stretched, my spine extended, and my body felt flexible and alive again. It is no wonder that many yoga postures are named after animals.

If there is a particular wound to attend to, you can call on animal guides to help you. First of all, take the attention to the wound. Then, with your intent, call or sing for an animal guide. If you are open to receive, an animal will come and help you. I call on animal guides a lot when working on other people. They are like eyes into places in the body I cannot see. They show me how the energy is blocked and what needs to be done to move it.

In order to work with animals, I have had to develop relationships with them, which at times has not been easy. There may be some kind of blockage or wound in the relationship between the animal and the human from the past which needs to be healed before the animals is open to human communication. At present, humans in general do not have good relations with animals because of the way we treat them. Consider, for example, the mouse again. The relationship between the mouse and the human is somewhat problematic at present. The human uses the mouse for experimentation and doesn't even eat them afterwards! Being eaten is literally fair game, and all the animal beings who come to Earth expect to be eaten sooner or later. It is the means by which their energy continues its movement through the universal body. Digestion is a magical transmuting process, which naturally moves the soul energy from one place to another in the dream of the universe. When the mouse is eaten by the snake, its energy moves through the snake star like, for example, blood moves from the top of the stomach to the groin. But humans do not even allow the mice to be eaten by insects and worms. After experimenting with them, they burn them. This is an incomplete transition. The fire only takes the mouse energy back to where it came, to its star, and the mouse hasn't completed its function on Earth. There is, in essence, a dysfunction in the system of the universal body.

This dysfunction is like a blood clot. If the energy does not move freely and efficiently through the universal body, the blood of the body slows down. The mouse moved within the natural processes of the universal body from the mouse star to planet Earth where it was supposed to be digested and transformed into another part of the universal body. By being sent back, it creates a kind of backlog of energy on the mouse star and intensifies the holding and heaviness of that idea. Thought needs to move quickly in order to maintain its creative flow. It is the same principle as mounting paperwork. If one part of the system isn't clear, another will suffer. Someone or something will not be getting the information they need in order to carry out their job properly. The mouse on Earth was meant for a snake or an eagle or a wild cat, not for a laboratory.

The mouse dreaming does not object to experimentation as such. Experimentation is part of the creative principle in the universal mind. But it is the clumsy manner in which modern humans carry out their experiments, which is causing the problem. Humans have been experimenting with animals harmlessly for years – through their dreaming. The shaman knows how to communicate with the mouse through the conscious dream, and the mouse, if duly respected, will give the shaman all the information that is necessary, freely and openly. It is more a friendly exchange. The human also has information that is useful to the mouse, and there is no reason for the shaman to withhold. We are dealing here with friendly and honest equal communication. These days when I travel to the mouse star, I have to take enormous gifts to apologise for the human ignorance. The mouse star, and all the information it holds, is pretty much off-limits these days to humans. This is a great loss. By not being able to touch a part of the universal body, we cannot touch a part of the Earth body, and we cannot touch a part of the human body. We are denied access to a part of ourselves.

Humans need to repair their relationship with the mouse. The first step is to stop all laboratory animal experimentation – NOW. The second step is to recreate links with their spirit through shamanic dreaming. The third step is a huge unconditional apology with very expensive gifts of time and energy. That should do the trick.

Animals are our guides through the universal body, the Earth body, and the human body. We need them.

SEVEN - THE PLANETARY BODY

At every stage of the breath from the very beginning, no energy could control entirely its own effect. As the first breath could not control the dreamers, the dreamers could not control the design, and now the design seed could not control its own growth. This is because the dreamers did not design in unison. They were not entirely aware of the other parts of themselves. The design seed tried to stabilise its ideas through repetition, and with some of its earlier concepts, this was successful, particularly with grasses and insects. But as it developed more compound extensions, so also it had to develop the truth of energy feeding on itself. Some parts of the crystal life would feed on other parts. It created new problems of balance within the planetary body. The seed saw in itself this dangerous yet necessary principle of growth. This was particularly difficult to control. The dinosaurs were the most extreme example of energy bodies that had grown too big for the main body to balance. It is said that a comet's collision with the planet Earth altered the elemental conditions to such an extent that the dinosaurs could no longer exist. But this was really a crude example of designer consciousness attempting to reassert some kind of control over its own body. Although the dinosaurs were a product of its seed, it was a product that had taken too much of a hungry will of its own and threatened to dominate the other aspects of the seed's growth. It was a *mark of how strong the dinosaurs had become that the larger aspects of design consciousness would go to such lengths in order to change so radically the surface of one of its planetary inheritances (investments).*

The planet Earth is a digestive organ in the universal body

Earth is a place of transformation. Everything that comes here does not leave in the same form. All forms are either transformed by the elemental process, as for example rocks are eroded by air, or by the principle of hunger. It could even be said that rocks are eaten by air. In the case of all microbes, plants and animals, it is clear that everything is eaten by something.

The more the dreamers invested themselves in their own dream and the more complex the intentions in the form, the further they got from the simplicity of the original breath.

The original breath comes directly from Soul, the essence of all. Nothing. The everything of nothing. Completion. An unconditional state of being. As soon as the designers began to mould the breath into matter, they created hunger. The essence of all phenomena is unconditional and entirely free of any intentions or purpose. The dreamers take this energy and use it in the grand experiment of the universe. They have created a tension. The individual soul knows the essence of its unconditional home. The further the individual soul travels into the universal mind-body, the greater will be the hunger for the return to the source. The first breath was unconditional, freely given, and this unconditional life, just for the love of it, is the Soul of all being. (There is a further definition of 'Soul' and 'individual soul' in chapter Nine.)

The further the dreamers developed their design, the more control was necessary to hold the design in fixed positions. From the elements came the bones of rock, and from crystal came the first microbes and simpler life forms. These forms were and are still closer to the place of the unconditional root, the first breath. Animals are more complex creatures and are further from the source. They have to come first through the dream of the elements and then through the cream of the crystal, DNA, microbes, plants. It is an interconnected thought process, a continuous dream in which everything comes from something. The elements are part of the mind that dreamed rocks. Elements and rocks are part of the mind that dreams crystal. Elements, rocks, and crystals are part of the mind that dreams DNA and the first microbes. The elements, rocks, crystal, DNA, microbes dream plants. The elements, rocks, crystal, DNA, microbes and plants dream animals.

The elements, rocks, crystal, DNA, microbes, plants and animals dream humans.

All along the line there is a sacrifice. The elements give themselves to rocks. Rocks give themselves to crystal. Crystals give themselves to microbes. Microbes give themselves to plants. Plants give themselves to animals. Animals give themselves to humans. The sacrifice is for the evolution of the dream of the universe. For the dream to evolve, complex forms will feed on simpler forms. It reminds me of a rhyme I learnt as a child. -

There was a young lady who swallowed a fly; perhaps she'll die.

There was a young lady who swallowed a spider. She swallowed a spider to catch the fly; perhaps she'll die.

There was a young lady who swallowed a mouse. She swallowed the mouse to catch the spider; she swallowed the spider to catch the fly, perhaps she'll die.

There was a young lady who swallowed a cat. She swallowed the cat to catch the mouse; she swallowed the mouse to catch the spider; she swallowed the spider to catch the fly, perhaps she'll die.

There was a young lady who swallowed a wolf. She swallowed the wolf to catch the cat; she swallowed the cat to catch the mouse; she swallowed the mouse to catch the spider; she swallowed the spider to catch the fly, perhaps she'll die.

There was a young lady who swallowed a man. She swallowed the man to catch the wolf; she swallowed the wolf to catch the cat; she swallowed the cat to catch the mouse; she swallowed the mouse to catch the spider; she swallowed the spider to catch the fly, perhaps she'll die.

There was a young lady who swallowed a dinosaur. . . . . .
. . . ..

When I was in the Amazon travelling with Ramon, a Peruvian shaman, (see my previous book 'Crystalhead'), he would always pray and make a small ceremony before he hunted. I asked him why.

"The animal sacrifices itself for me. I have to respect its spirit or it will harm my stomach."

What is sacrifice? The giving of the life of oneself so that

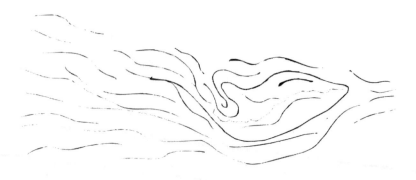

another can live. It is the ultimate act of love. Animals pass through the pain of death so that we can live. The pain is the same as the pain you would feel if you gave your life for someone. There is a part of you that would override the natural instincts of your body to survive.

We are all part of the same mind, all part of the same being - rock, animal, human. We are all part of a dream that learns through its own experiments. On some level, animals have given of themselves to humans. They are in a sense our direct parents. The trees are our grandparents. The rocks are our great grandparents. Children don't always behave and no doubt some animals, trees and rocks would rather they hadn't given themselves to the human to develop the dream further. Growth is painful. The pain an animal feels when it dies is a testament to the growing pains of the universe. If you want to evolve, a part of you has to die. It is the law of change. We are the result of this evolution and it is entirely interconnected. There is no separation between man and nature. Everything is natural. A human is as natural as a tree.

Here is a fundamental difference between the shamanic worldview and the materialist worldview. The shaman understands that everything is interconnected and is part of the same being. The materialist tends to see the physical world as something to use. When the Eastern Mexican indigenous tribes found that the Spanish mestizos had built a huge railway through the huricuta, they were outraged. Had the spirits of the land been asked first? The land is alive, living, breathing, being. The Soul is everywhere - in the mountains, the trees, and the insects. As far as the tribes were concerned, the Spanish did not respect the Mother. As far as the Spanish were concerned, the tribes did not respect God!

For the Mexican indigenous tribes, the Earth is the mother because it is closer to the source. They re-trace their connection with the divine mother through the Earth. The great landscape of the Earth dream contains so many keys and doorways. The restless urge that so many of us have to travel is the individual soul hunting for clues to re-connect with home. Unlike the tribes who keep their traditions, the white urban humans suffer from a deep alienation from this source. They have lost the sense of the divine parents in the land who hold us like children. The clues are in the land on which the body walks. Every aspect of the landscape is like an active symbol, which opens up to reveal its part in the movement of soul energy. We may be drawn irresistibly to a particular mountain, a river, a tree, a beach, and a country. The journey is like connecting with a part of us we have forgotten. It is like trying to find our way home. The resonance of a particular part of the Earth awakens a deep truth in ourselves.

Gradually, as we open to different parts of the Earth dream, their connections are revealed. The dream teaches us how energy moves through all the forms. All is interconnected. From animal to tree to grass to flower to stone office block. Everything is energy; everything is part of the dream, and despite the illusion that forms are separated, there is an invisible web of energy that weaves its way through all surfaces.

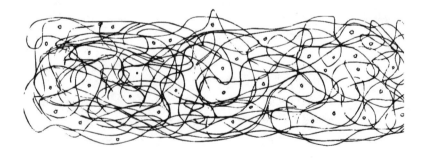

I remember the first time I experienced this sense of interconnectedness. I was on the beautiful West Coast of

Ireland, sharing a cottage with my (human!) mother. One day we were walking on the beach. We had drifted a little apart, both of us meditating in our own ways. Looking out to sea, I saw the water dissolve into tiny globules of energy. I felt my sight being drawn into the sea through the surface. As I looked deeper into it, I could see the changes of quality in the tiny globules, which appeared like diagrams of atoms. As my head was lifted out of the sight of the sea, I was looking then into the sky. I could see the difference between qualities of globules, a different atomic structure. My eyes were taken onto the land. Again, I was taken into the molecules of energy that vibrate on the surface and deep into the cliffs and under the fields. The energy in the land had the same sense of minute particles but with a different quality to the sea and a different quality to the sky. My mother came walking towards me. Another molecular structure! I could see her energy in the energy of the land on which she walked and the energy of the air offset by the energy of the sea. It was incredible to see a human glowing in the context of all the other energy around her.

All is energy, tiny molecules vibrating at different rates of the Earth vibration.

When the eyes see through the surface of separated forms to the web of energy that interconnects all spaces, the conscious dreamer can expand their attention into the universal dream. The energy that vibrates in land, sea and sky, extends to other planets, other stars, other galaxies. The web of energy in one dream links with the web of energy in another; the dream of the Earth links with the dream of Venus, the dream of Mars, of Neptune, of Sirius. The conscious dreamer can open to all the interconnecting dream spaces of the mind.

EIGHT - HUMANS

(This section of 'speak' refers to the next three chapters.)

Another problem for the dreamers was that although they conceived of the planets, and were responsible for the principles under which they evolved, they could not control the planetary evolution itself. The planets had already evolved their own sense of innate movement, which was beyond the direct control of the dreamers. So when the dreamers took the step of injecting their seed into the planets, they were to some extent inheriting a body which already had an independent history. So many of the problems experienced by the seed of the dreamers were in trying to understand the planetary body in which it was planted. The dreamers were very imperfect magicians who did not have full control over their own magic. They were not entirely unified. They were not entirely aware of the other parts of the whole. The dinosaurs were a gross result of the dreamers' crystal seed attempting to combine effectively with the elemental planetary body. The sudden and dramatic demise of the dinosaurs, together with every other species that has overstepped the mark of the dreamers' will, is well preserved in the memory of the planetary body.

The main tension between the planet Earth and the crystal design seed is one of pace. The dreamers always want to go faster than the planet because essentially the dreamers think before they feel. (The planet was after all originally designed by the same consciousness that seeks a greater pace of change.) The Earth has its own way and its own time, and it suffers all the fall-out from the dreamers' experiments. It has to absorb the principle of death, which allows the dreamers to keep trying. The dreamers have a problem because the various individual parts, which grow from the crystal seed, do not have the same vision as the seed itself. The creations of the dreamers are not willing to be merely part of a grand experiment. They value their life for itself. The planet itself also only knew its own life; it did not have the external presence of the early dreamers whose consciousness extended into all aspects of the universe. The pain absorbed by the planet would always be far greater than the dreamers who could still jump outside to the relative indifference of the observer.

These were some of the problems facing the dreamers. To deal with them, they invested more of their energy into the planet. They came, as it were, a second time, and planted a seed within the first seed that had developed into all the various forms thus far. Their intention this time was to make a mirror, something that would reflect themselves more completely so they could experience life on Earth to a greater depth. This time they planted more crystal, but a particular crystal with a particular energy. They planted the crystal skull.

The crystal skull was the birth of humanity. From the intention of the form planted in the planet, the human would develop through its various forms into a body that could hold the memory of the dreamers themselves. The dreamers in planting the crystal skull had sown the seed for the manifestation of their own reflection to be born on this planet. The human would not only come from the seed, but would develop the same awareness as the seed itself. The intention with the placing of the crystal skull was to make designed humans as human designers. The dreamers wanted to see themselves on Earth.

The human reflects the dreamer

Unlike every other material being on planet Earth, the human can travel to any place in the universe. The dreaming body of the human can extend as far as the minds of the dreamers themselves. The human can travel to the spaces in the universe where the different animals are located. They can be part of the creative mind of the universe. The potential of the human mind is no less than the potential of the dreamers of the universe. That is the depth of our responsibility.

Human Teachers of the Dream

As the dreaming body expands, the spaces open, and these new experiences can be daunting. For this reason, we need interpreters, human teachers of the dream who help us to move through the different dimensions of the universe.

The human teachers of the universal dream give instructions on where to go and what to do. They are the councillors and healers. They have the wide perspective that an individual can never have, and so they are the guides through spaces of confusion and unknowing. The skill of human teachers of the universal dream is to show us how we can gradually expand our consciousness from the place of our human body, through the dream of the Earth, to the universal dream.

There are many different guides, and each guide has a particular purpose and deals with a particular aspect of the universal dream. One of the first guides I had was a North American Indian. He came to me slowly, gradually, in brief glimpses at first like a noticeable face in a crowd, and then with more regularity. He would appear, usually when I was meditating, and then look at me, and that was all.

Meditating has been for me one of the most effective ways of connecting to the different layers of the universal dream. I have tried many methods, but the one that tends to suit me is simply sitting and breathing naturally without any intention, and trying to accept without any judgement whatever it is I am feeling or thinking. In time, when the thoughts gradually settle, (sometimes with a lot of patience!) the dream opens. I am ready to receive.

The guide came to me and sat with me and looked into my eyes. I felt as though he was teaching me something that I didn't understand. I was very deferential at first and didn't ask anything of him. I just looked back, interested, but not knowing what it was I was looking into or for. I liked him being there and

I felt like a young student waiting for instruction.

After some years, the dreaming of this guide changed and I was taken – dreamed – into a desert landscape. It was a familiar desert to me, Mexican, but I had never been to this exact place that the dream was taking me. Across the desert plain, I could see a horse. On the horse was a male figure that kept changing from a Mexican Indian to a North American Indian. The man appeared like a changing cubist painting, never holding his form for very long. He got off his horse, and he looked at me.

That look. Those eyes. They were like the eyes of the guide I had seen all these years, but they were dancing, alive. That desert land was dancing and alive. I noticed stones, incredible rocks. I bent down to look closer at the desert land. He was saying to me, without speaking, that the more fixed I could see the detail on the dreamscape, the greater would be my understanding, and the greater the dexterity in the Art of Seeing. In the dreamscape no object is irrelevant. All shapes and forms contain energy and power and it is the job of the dreamer to feel them. The guide directed me to a rock. Great rock. In the dream I was directed to touch the rock. Real. Touch. A touch or reality. I was alive. For the first time in my life. I felt it – life. The rock in that dream engaged my attention so completely, I felt as if I had landed. It was as if my soul beforehand was floating around my body without entering into it. I could feel my physical body was at one with my soul. This great teacher was showing a sense of depth in the Earth dream that didn't seem imaginable. The rock was alive. I was alive.

The dream opens up by degrees. Each time we return to the same dream, a little more is discovered. Gradually, the relations between different aspects of the dream become clearer.

I returned many times to the same dream, the feeling of those dancing eyes that shifted everything in my body. I felt as though I was going somewhere without knowing where. I was excited and frightened, but my curiosity was always greater than my fear. I felt as if I was being trained for something. By learning to hold the attention of the dancing eyes, my dreaming body was developing, becoming accustomed to being in a new place that seemed to have a different vibration from the world I was used to. The physical body acclimatises. Slowly. After a while, it can open up a little more to another part of the Great Mystery.

The guide led me across the desert to a glass dome that looked like a large greenhouse. Inside, it looked dense with green. I walked through the door and no sooner had I smelt the dense plant life, a flock of white birds suddenly rushed out of the door into the empty blue skies. The dome was left entirely empty. Empty of plants, empty of birds. My body felt heat. Everywhere. And love. Incredible love.

In all these scenes I had to accept a level of unknowing. On the level of gut sensation everything made complete sense. But I couldn't begin to explain or analyse. As soon as I tried, I got a really bad headache. Trying to understand too quickly with my intellect was like trying to grip something too large to hold. Like a child, I had to learn to accept being guided, which meant I had to let go of control, and this for me was very difficult. I had a lot of fights with myself. I am a man not a boy, I would remonstrate. But it really didn't help. I couldn't dream when I wasn't accepting. So I had to learn to let go, release, accept, and trust. And then the guide would take me further.

On the desert plain, I was shown a triangle, a white triangle. It was as big as a two-storey building, and it shone. I felt fear and I felt fascination. The guide was encouraging me to go through. But I wasn't sure. I really wasn't sure.

When does the child become a man? When he has control? But how can he take control if he doesn't know anything? In the material world, I was a man, in this dreaming, I was a boy. The man was suspicious, the boy adventurous.

"How do you know the guide isn't using you," says the man.

"I want to see what is on the other side, " shouts the boy.

"You could go mad messing around with this kind of stuff," says the man.

"I don't want to be stuck here all my life," shouts the boy.

And the boy leads the reluctant man like the son must guide the frightened father through the white triangle to the other side.

The other side. This is the dance. This is where the eyes move me, the body tingling, the colours flowing through, the creative play, energy, sustained ecstasy. The white triangle is a doorway to other worlds, and I explore the endless beauty. Pleasure. Real pleasure.

It was a real pleasure to meet this Indian guide. I was shown how beyond the white triangle are other triangles that make a very intricate construction, and each triangle is another doorway to another reality. It is a very fluid world and my physical body found it very hard to sustain my attention there. My meditations became exercises in sustained attention.

It felt as if my body was being trained to survive these different vibrational layers of the dream. Many times I felt overwhelmed by the power of the energy which passed through me. The guide showed me how to focus on the second chakra area, which is just above the groin and below the navel, and to focus on an upward pointing triangle. This holds the energy in the power centre of the body and stabilises the energy body so that there is enough strength to function in the dream. I spent many hours over some years passing through the white triangle on the desert floor, happy to explore these ecstatic layers of the dream.

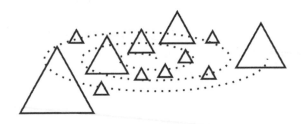

But some time after the elation of this discovery, the guide made it very clear to me that pleasure was not the only point of this exercise. He took me one day through the white triangle, and I found myself swirling down into the mouth of a whale, and the whale itself was swirling in a sea vortex that drew us deep down into the ocean. The whale disappears, and I am standing on the bottom of an ocean. I swing slowly like seaweed in the waves, and like an uprooted leaf, I drift in the tide towards something on the ocean floor. There seems to be the curved tops of walls, like an ancient city, the rest having been long since buried, and the walls of this place are in the shape of a cross. I am attracted to the point where the two arms of the cross meet and I feel like I am being held by two arms that extend from the sides of the cross. I feel the arms draw me towards the cross like the mother drawing me to the womb, and when I feel I am at the meeting place of the cross, I try and feel my back through it. I am using my intent, my will, to go through this image. I try to push with my back with all my strength through the vision, and from the arms of the cross appears a triangle. A white triangle. I am looking at the white triangle that rises from the arms of the cross at the bottom of the ocean. I am looking at the white triangle that rises from the brown desert floor. I see a white triangle that forms in space from the stars. I am in three places, and they are all one.

My body felt as if I had moved somewhere else. I didn't think it was possible to go beyond the worlds on the other side of the white triangle, but this experience had engaged my body in a way that felt like a further shift. My training now was to understand these three different layers of the dream. The bottom of the sea where so many of the secrets of this planet are held, the stars, and the desert. The desert was the place where the Earth and the stars could meet through my dreaming body. I returned to all these parts of the dream many times to understand how my dreaming body can span such huge distances. My guide was teaching me how this was possible.

It was, I was learning, a question of perspective. My physical body, like any other part of the Earth dream, is a doorway, an opening to other aspects of the dream. In my body are not only bones, blood and tissue, but also seas, mountains, and stars. There are invisible energy lines in the physical body that corresponds to the relation between all parts of the dream. From my physical body, my dreaming body could expand into nothing less than the whole universe.

I got to a stage in our relationship where I began to speak directly to the guide. I started to ask questions, and sometimes I got very clear answers. I began to feel that this guide wanted me to do something for him, or with him, and I needed to be sure of myself in the dream in order to achieve this. Our relationship, then, was becoming more adult, but if I was no longer the boy, I was still the apprentice.

The dream moved again, when in one dream, I went through the white triangle and there was me. My head and my body. I was looking at myself, the only body in a black space, and I could see myself being carried yet I couldn't see the carrier. I saw myself in a bed of light and there was an operation being conducted on my stomach, which has always been my physical weakness. The Indian guide was telling me sternly –

"Go beyond the self. Go beyond the self."

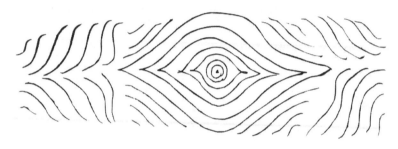

I could see and feel the passionate urgency in his eyes. I raised myself up from the bed of light. I raised myself from this whole world of light. I moved behind myself into a space of unknowing. I had no idea where I was going; I just followed the sense of where the eyes of my guide were taking me. Eventually, I arrived on a plain as flat as ice and as blue as the desert sky. There were crowds of people coming towards me, and one of them, a woman, held me with her blue eyes. They were incredible, those eyes, of youth and of age, of maiden and grandmother. They were so powerful, I could barely hold up my head, but the Indian guide was giving me strength with his intent. I became a channel that was directing energy from his eyes, through her eyes, and up to this incredible land I could glimpse and feel but could not possibly describe. I could feel the guide coming through the stages I had been through

– the space of self, the place of light, the flat plain of blue, and through the eyes of the dreaming woman, he was directing his attention through me, like the birds from the dome, up and away.

What was going on? I knew that the guide was using my attention now, and I wanted to know why. What was his purpose? I asked him directly – what do you want of me?

He took me to the United States of America, to the old battlefields where many of his tribe had perished. He showed me their wounds and he showed me their pain. Their pain wasn't that they were dead, their pain was that they were still on that field, even though their physical bodies had died. The guide explained to me that by focusing his attention through my dreaming body he could lead the trapped souls to the grandmother that I had met on the star blue dreaming plains. It was here that the whole tribe would collect and dream their future. They didn't want to move on until all the tribe had successfully left the Earth material realm. Their dreaming, he explained, is like a ship in time and space, and he didn't want to leave before all the tribe had gathered. He needed to use my Earth body to re-connect with these souls and bring them home. I was a kind of bridge over which they would pass.

He took me back to the white dome in the desert. I saw again the white birds flying out into the blue skies.

"These are the souls that you are releasing." He said.

I didn't understand. What is a trapped soul?

As so often happens with human teachers of the dream, my guide didn't explain in words but he gave me a sense, just by looking at me. I saw that the dreamer doesn't only intend the soul into the Earth dream. The Earth dream is one of many dreams within the whole universal dream, like different parts of the whole. When the soul is dreamed into the Earth, it passes through the whole elemental process – through Air, Fire, Earth and water – thought, passion, body, emotion. This dream of the Earth is like a full out-breath before the in-breath returns the energy to source. A trapped soul is like an uncompleted dream. Trapped souls have not completed the breath of their life on Earth. They are like genies in bottles waiting for conscious dreamers to help them move on and continue their journey.

For the first time in my conscious dreaming life, I was presented with all the facts. For the first time, I had a full choice. Technically, I could say no. And this for me, seemed almost like a rite of passage. The right to say no! Technically, at any rate. In truth, by this time, my heart was so committed; I felt I had to complete this part of the work. I gave myself to this guide and allowed him to work through me. I learnt through his eyes how to make a clear passage from the Earth plane to the star blue dreaming plane of the grandmother. My body felt very hot during this process and at times I wondered if it could contain the energy that was moving through. But it did, and it does, and I have learned through this guide how much trapped soul energy there is on this planet, not just from his tribe. At least now I know there is something we can do about it.

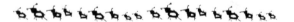

The North American guide also helps in understanding animal guides. I had a proliferation of ants at one time, particularly in my stomach, and I didn't know why. I asked the guide for advice and he showed me how ants get into the tiniest cracks in the Earth surface, and in the same way they could show me the tiniest details of the dream. I have a long-standing problem with my stomach and so I used the ants to journey into the intricate levels of the digestive dream to see what was going on. The dreaming bodies of the ants seem to know how to survive there.

Another time, my animal guide was a very hungry and angry big cat, like a leopard. It just wanted to eat anything, so huge was its hunger. The guide told me to watch the animal, and I would learn the roots of my desire.

Also this guide brings me gifts, usually stones. Two stones to be precise. One is always blue and the other is white or green. These are healing stones, which I must learn to use in relation to various parts of the body.

A relationship with a guide doesn't happen overnight. It takes many years to mature and to develop understanding. You can return to an aspect of a dream at will if you remember it well enough. Then your relation with the dream teacher can develop depth. A dream teacher can be called up simply by projecting your intention into the dream, or by calling by name if there is a name. But by the same token, a dream teacher can call you up, and sometimes they don't wait until you are nice and comfortable in your dreaming position. You could be driving your car or sitting on the loo and there they are, teaching as the shit drops.

The Dalai Lama

The Dalai Lama came to me on a train. I was in Java, Indonesia, travelling between Jakarta and Surabaya, where I was taking part in a movement course. I was in a pretty sad way, suffering a lot of grief over a broken relationship and feeling very low. Alone. I was crying on the night train between Jakarta and Surabaya. It was one of those times when I couldn't see any light or any guides; I could only see my own sadness. My body felt incredibly heavy and it had given in completely. Despair is an opening. A trauma is an opening. The resistance of the body and mind is no longer there, and this is an opening. An opportunity.

All of a sudden in the carriage there was a light, incredibly bright, flickering around, jumping around the carriage. The Dalai Lama was sitting on the luggage rack high on the other side of the carriage. I burst out laughing. I woke the person next to me (so sorry). And then the Dalai Lama was on the roof. Smiling. I felt such love, such complete love. The feeling came from nowhere. My heart was open and totally believing.

He moved my head towards the seat in front of me. My brother David was there. He had died of cancer a year earlier at the age of 35. He was as real as the person I had woken earlier. He was smiling in his matter-of-fact kind of way. David was always incredibly logical.

"Are you all right?" I said.

"Yes. I'm fine." He said.

And he was. I knew he was. There was no doubt that he was. He was smiling at me in that arrogant kind of way he has, as if seeing someone alive who was dead was the most natural thing in the world, and why should I bother to even be remotely surprised?

"I'm going now," he said.

Well why not, there was nothing else to say or know. Death is life and life is death. I saw him like he had just stepped outside the house to go for a casual walk, and maybe he would come back one day, and maybe not, and one day I would also go for a walk to have a look round the neighbourhood. Why not? Something to do.

"Ok," I said. It felt entirely natural. And he went. And so I know that David, despite all the incredible pain he had suffered, was really ok. And I felt incredibly happy.

The Dalai Lama called me back. There was more he wanted to show me. I sat up. He wanted me to meditate on the different chakras. He said I should start at the base. I meditated on the base chakra and saw this shape –

He told me to move upwards. At the second chakra, I saw this shape –

At the third chakra, I was shown

At the fourth chakra, the heart

At the fifth chakra, the throat

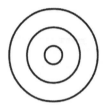

At the sixth chakra on the temple

And at the seventh chakra at the top of the head

"Meditate on these, he said. "They will teach you."

For the next year, I meditated on these shapes. I found that they were an elaboration of what the American Indian guide had taught me. Each chakra is a different form of stabilised energy and I could learn how to relate to the energy of the whole universal dream from different areas of my body. In many ways, it was a teaching of how to ground the often abstracted nature of the universal dream comprehensively into physical experience. I could experience the dream through my whole body. I was learning that my physical body could be moved by the dreaming body.

I could develop this understanding of the dreaming body with Surprapto Suryodarmo, the Amerta movement teacher (with a physical body!). He showed me how the human body reads the language of other bodies and energies. The human body is a complete channel and can extend itself to relate to all other energy forms. It was during this course that we visited Borrobadur, the largest Buddhist monument in the world, and I learnt that many Tibetan lamas come here because much of their teaching originated in the land that is now called Indonesia. So my dreaming on the train was an opening to a deep memory and connection in the land which had been established for centuries.

The memory of the human body connects with the memory held in the planetary body. As the human walks the land, the land transmits the wisdom it holds through the feet. This triggers the collective memory held in the body of every human, so we can feel in a foreign place that our experience is incredibly familiar. In truth every human has been everywhere that all humans have been. We have access to the complete collective consciousness of humanity. It is stored in our memory. By walking the land we awaken our memory. The body of the human is an enormous library waiting to be read, and different places on the globe hold different keys to certain important books on the shelves. Everything that was ever known is held in the body. And a whole encyclopaedia can be read in a matter of moments.

There is an energy transmission that is a lot more efficient than words. A rock can teach this.

The Australian Aboriginals

Uluru is a particularly powerful rock. The great monolith in the centre of Australia had been calling me from Indonesia. Aboriginal boy guides had been entering my dreaming in Java and showing me sand paintings. I couldn't completely understand them. In general they seemed to be indicating a place from which to take off. I followed the dream to Australia. I met some Aboriginals in Darwin who taught me how to negotiate the incredibly ancient dreaming of that land. I hadn't felt anything like it and really at times felt out of my depth. There were some energies which were particularly powerful forms. They spun my dreaming body into complete unknowing. The Aboriginals taught me to call on the stars for help. I called on the energy of the plaeiades because I had been connecting with them in Indonesia and there seemed to be a lot of light (sight) coming from them. In Australia the relationship between the stars and the land does not feel very distant. I could connect my dreaming body with the stellar energy and this would help me to see into the great deep caves of the dreaming in that land. For the Aboriginals, there is a continuum of the land to the stars and the stars to the land. It is all one dream. It is the paradise of the dreamweavers who have sung their song through the spaces of the whole universal body. The Aboriginals gave me permission to enter the caves of their dreaming, and they gave me protection.

Uluru holds the earliest records of human experience. So

much of it is secret and so much of it has to remain secret. The history of the white man in Australia is a catalogue of intolerance and abuse. The value system of the white man is so different from the Aboriginals it is a wonder they come from the same seed. The Aboriginals say that when the white man is ready, he will be shown some of the real teachings of their dream. The small amount they told me I am not able to relate yet. We have to respect a secret until it is time for it to sing.

A word or two about secrets. They are frustrating and seem unnecessary. I really hate them, and in almost all my attempts to connect with shamanic teachers there has always been an aura of secrecy and the question of whether I could be trusted to keep them. The reason for this is obvious: abuse. A secret usually holds power and power is almost always abused. A secret is also a delicate piece of the soul. It is the heart of the soul and should be treated as one would treat the deepest feelings of your lover. For these reasons I have reluctantly had to learn to keep them, and so I am trusted more. I don't think that secrets are desirable, they are a burden mostly. But my curiosity is such that I will take them on. Most of the time, innocence is bliss, and if innocence is a cat, then curiosity definitely killed mine!

But we can sing the song of Uluru. There is at that rock a beautiful dream and a beautiful secret. The Aboriginals know the source of light that dreams the rocks and dreams the animals and weaves them with the stars. Theirs is a gift beyond time. I look forward to the day when the whole of humanity is ready to learn from them.

Teachers of the dream, teachers of the planet. Energy lines under the surface connect one land to another. The tail of the crocodile extends from the heart of Australia through the whole of South East Asia. There is no learning that is separate. Every tribe of each land holds a piece of the whole dream.

The Dalai Lama (again)

I was led again to the Dalai Lama. It had been a year since he appeared to me in the train. I had meditated on the shapes I had been shown at each chakra and now it was time to go further. I went to Nepal to meditate. I found a monastery in the hills above Kathmandu. In one of the temples of this monastery blessed by a thousand Buddhas, the Dalai Lama continued his instruction.

I was shown in more detail how the etheric structures of the body combine. Each chakra relates to another chakra in an architectural way that is very precise. Day by day the edifice of the etheric body was constructed, and I was shown how the individual structure relates to the continuum. The intricacies of the structure I perceived showed the joining of all the chakras into one frame. This frame is strong enough to hold the more powerful and potentially overwhelming areas of the dream. This was not easy. At each meditation I had to let go of an aspect of my individual or separated self to understand how I am an energy structure within energy structures; how I am one stone brick in an infinite palace. I had to let go of my ego in order to see the incredible power in the beauty of the design. I had to see my chakra as the chakra; my body as the body; my energy as the energy. I got so far and then I felt saturated with learning. My desires were screaming. I have never felt such extremes of lust, hate, love, hunger, anger, sadness, bliss and despair all in a day. It was as close to madness as I had ever been. If this was attachment to the ego, then I confess, I was very attached. There was a lot more I had to let go of before I could continue my instructions with his holiness. In all humility, I blessed that Tibetan dream, and then sought comfort in the distractions of Kathmandu.

The North American Indian and Tibetan guides are the most popular with the clients I work with. I think this is because the level of attention in the dreaming of these two nations is so well developed and held. I believe in the case of the Tibetan Buddhist dream, their holding on the land caused their demise. The exclusive theocracy that grew around the monasteries of the high mountains created a protectorate for the jewels of their dreams like a castle that was just inviting a conqueror. In many ways, the Chinese conquest has been a gift because the Tibetans, in order to survive, have been force to display many (but by no means all) the wonders of their understanding of the dream to the spiritually starving nations of the 'developed' world. And how the materialist consciousness of the west has fed on the knowledge of the high mountains!

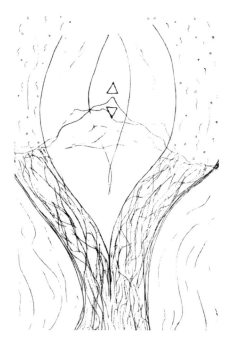

The Priestess and the Empress

I tend to meet the feminine presence in connection with particular places on the land. The strongest presence of the feminine principle I have felt is at Glastonbury, England, at Chalice Well. Here is a spirit which is so palpable, I feel like I enter into her 'body'. My whole body feels warm every time I walk into her presence; she is incredibly wise and kind. I sit by the well with my notepad and I ask her questions, usually about problems I have with clients or with my love life! Her answers are always so crisp and clear. I don't doubt a word she says and sometimes will channel the information directly to the client feeling completely confident (even if I don't understand completely what is being said) that on some level the client will gain insight from her wisdom. I have found with channelling that I have to forget who I am to give the energy a clear passage. The energy at Chalice Well is very much the energy of the Priestess in the tarot. Reflective, receptive, lunar.

At high lakes like Lago Atitlan in Guatemala and Lake Batur in Bali, the priestess is also strong. It has a different quality to Glastonbury. Glastonbury is more down to Earth and direct. These energies of the high lakes are more expansive. Her beauty is almost too much, and I find myself being able to do little else but wander around in open-mouthed wonder. Active volcanoes, like protectors, surround both these lakes. Perhaps it is this protection which allows her to relax into that kind of misty whiteness. Is it possible, this beauty? Yes it is possible. It is here on planet Earth.

The Empress of the tarot I have felt mostly at a beach in North Wales. The sense here has a raw no-nonsense power that suffers no fools and will only show the information if and when you are ready. It was she who told me to go to Peru, and only if I found something would she reveal more. I didn't even know what the something was until I got to Mexico (after Peru). It was a feeling, a kind of jewel hidden inside. When I returned to the beach, she begrudgingly led me deeper into her chambers of triangular rooms inside rooms, all going deeper and deeper into the ocean.

She gave me things, showed me things. Things I wouldn't know how to explain and wouldn't know if it was right to explain. The kind of things that just makes you feel like you've got it, after all this time, it was staring you in the face – I mean, how dumb can you be? Symbols, signs, colour, and feelings, which make complete sense in one moment. At least there is one moment's peace.

The Protector, Jesus and Merlin

There are other teachers I have encountered also. There is a protector, an African man, who will not allow me to reveal his name. The effectiveness of his protection depends upon the degree to which I believe in his powers of protection. This is true of all dream teachers. They feed, as it were, on belief. The more I believe in them, the more real they become, and the more they actually function for me or through me. In fact, the whole journey of the conscious dreamer is a journey of belief. It is not exactly blind faith because there are clear indications that the dream teachers exist. For me, feeling is the main test. By feeling I mean a sensing in the whole of my body if something is real or not. My body knows the truth of a presence; it cannot confuse in the way my intellect can. I only trust completely my direct experience. The body knows, the body knows, there is nothing that the body has not known.

Jesus is a guide also. I have problems with the concept of Jesus because I was brought up a Roman Catholic and believing in Jesus meant having to go to church on Sunday and various other rules and laws. But I accepted Jesus as a guide in Jerusalem. I visited the three main religious sites in Jerusalem: the dome of the rock, the church of the Holy Sepulchre, and the Wailing Wall. I felt the power of Allah, I felt the power of Jesus, and I felt the power of Yahweh. All the parts of the same, and the ridiculous arguments that echo around the world are lame semantic excuses for simple tribal warfare. There's nothing quite like a good old enemy.

The most intriguing guide I have encountered is Merlin. I talk about him more in chapter 11. Sometimes I think Merlin is all my guides mixed together. It is impossible to have a conversation with him. He is much too quick for the incredibly ponderous medium of words. He prefers colour movement, sign. Giving my body and vision to this guide is like seeing backwards, or sideways. I can't explain, but I know, the body just knows. There is no question. To most this is blind faith. To me it feels like real sight.

It is a curious paradox that we have to let go of knowing in order to know.

Exercise 12. **Conscious Dreaming**
Connecting with Dream Teachers

This exercise follows all the steps of the first Conscious Dreaming exercise in chapter six. The only addition is that a prayer or song is very necessary. You can make your own prayer. Here is a suggestion.

Great Spirit, I open my heart to your teaching. I ask for guidance. I ask to meet my guide who will help me on this path. Teach me through this dream, how to connect to my guide. Help me to open to receive.

To begin with, a breath awareness meditation will help to create the space you need. Then sing to the guide, or call in words, or open your heart silently to your teachers. Teachers will come into the dream when you are ready to receive them. The most you can do is to be ready and open. They may take you on a journey. As the dreaming body travels, use your out-breath to project your energy through the dream space, and use your in-breath to draw in the energy you need to travel. The in-breath is the fuel, the out-breath the motor.

A teacher will often appear in a dream during sleep. A meditation practise can open the spaces of the mind, but it doesn't mean that a teacher will appear on cue. It could happen at any time, and then you can listen to the voices that have been trying to connect with you for so long.

When a teacher has made him or herself known, perhaps through a vision, perhaps through a sound, a word, a feeling, there is a bit more to go on. You can then consciously call up the energy of the teacher and spend time getting to know them more. You can ask questions, but the answers may not be in the form that you expect. It can take great patience in your listening to develop trust and a sense of who your teacher is, and what you have to learn from them. Faith is a key to your progress. A total belief in yourself, the truth of your experience, the intuitive wisdom and knowledge that you hold.

Chakras

Chakras are the means through which our physical body relates to our dreaming body. We extend from the physical into the material and non-material dream through these energetic doorways. As the ability to dream consciously is developed, the chakras become increasingly important as a means of orientation in the dream, and as a means of understanding the relation with different dream spaces.

Base Chakra Meditation

To start the chakra meditation, feel the four elements in your body. The breath, the temperature, the feelings of your bones, and the mass of water in your body. The four elements are part of the symbol of the base chakra. Through the base chakra, ground the awareness of the body into the place where you sit. The symbol of the base chakra strengthens the relation between the human body and the Earth body. It is the means by which we orientate ourselves in relationship to the eight principle directions on our compass.

Line of Air:

Line of Fire:

Line of Earth:

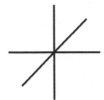

Line of Water:

The elements find their place in the eight directions and the body is grounded through the base chakra.

This is where I am
This is my body

This is where I sit
This is my place
Now.

The magic of the breath and the attention of the mind connect the human body to the Earth planetary body through this symbol.

The breath is the means by which energy can be moved into and through the chakra areas of the body. The base chakra is the first entrance point of Earth energy. To access this energy, take the attention with the out-breath deep into the planet. When you have sensed the planet Earth energy, breathe the energy up with your in-breath. With the in-breath, draw the energy from the Earth into the base chakra. This can be an incredibly invigorating experience. Many people feel heat or strong energy in their base chakra. The energy can be a little overwhelming, so it is wise to bring it up a little at a time to begin with.

As you open more to Earth planet energy, your dreaming body is joined with the planet. The Earth human body consciously extends into the Earth planetary energy. The illusory boundaries of the sense of self are dissolved, and the Earth planetary body lives through your breath.

Exercise 13. **Second Chakra Meditation**

The second chakra is the place of our power. The symbol of the second chakra is the triangle.

The second chakra is the place where the power of the Earth body projects out from the human body. The resonance of the triangle is the means through which this power is projected from the human body into the universal dream. It is a reference point; it holds us to the human body and the Earth body. From this clear place of orientation, other areas of the universal dream can be mapped.

The American Indian guide was teaching me how the Earth dream is so much greater than what it appears to be. He showed me how there is such a wealth of experience beneath the surface of our perceptions, our pleasures and our pains. When we have developed our full attention to all aspects of the Earth dream – the elements, trees, plants, flowers, animals, humans, the interconnecting landscape – we are able to travel with strength through other parts of the universal dream. If we are not fully grounded in the Earth dream, and we attempt to travel through the universal mind, we are in danger of losing our sense of who we are, the place of our perspective. We need to develop the strength in our Earth dream so as not to lose ourselves, which can result in confusion and loss of energy.

The focus of the triangle strengthens the connection with the Earth dream. It is the place from which one can be held in the large spaces of the universal dream. A home base. It is always possible to return to the consciousness of the body through the doorway of the triangle, so with this in mind, one is never lost. With the breath, it is always possible to move your dreaming body within the dream. This prevents being stuck somewhere we don't know or understand. By co-ordinating the breath with the attention on this shape, safe interaction with all areas of the universal mind can be achieved.

To strengthen your connection with this chakra symbol, use the breath in co-ordination with the base chakra. With the in-breath, draw up the energy from the planet Earth into and through the base chakra. With the out-breath, direct the energy out through the second chakra. The power of the Earth energy will be felt moving through you. Almost everyone I have worked with is frightened of the power that comes through the base and second chakras. Many world religions are devoted to repressing the Earth spirit energies. The repression comes from a place of fear. Fear is a constant enemy of the conscious dreamer. The courage of the warrior is needed to overcome the fear of the powerful Earth energies that can move through us. It is only energy, and we need all the energy we can get.

Exercise 14. **Third Chakra Meditation**

The third chakra is the opening up to the animal part of our being.

It is the place of 'gut reaction'. Our animal instinct. Through this chakra we communicate with the animal body in the human. Through this chakra we also communicate with all other animal bodies on the planet. It is the place of fear and hunger and survival. The frightened animal will close this chakra; the bold animal will open it. If it is closed, the animal starves, if it is open, the animal can hunt effectively.

The opening of the solar plexus chakra is in itself an act of facing our fear. The energy is drawn in with the in-breath and feeds the seat of power in the second chakra. It gives strength to the dreaming animal body.

The third chakra is an opening. Breathe in animal strength and fearlessness through the solar plexus and, with the out-breath, ground and resolve the strength through the second chakra.

A particular powerful breathing meditation is to breathe in through both the base and solar plexus chakras – Earth power and animal strength – and then to breathe the energy out through the power centre of the second chakra.

Exercise 15. **Fourth Chakra Meditation**

The fourth chakra is the meeting place of the Earth body

And the dreamers of the universe.

The meeting forms the six-pointed star.

It is through the heart chakra that the dialogue between the dreamers and the human Earth body is developed. The ancestral dreamers are the core of the energy that dreams us. The dreamed Earth body reaches out through the heart to the greater consciousness in the rest of the universal dream. The dreamed body connects to the dreamer and can feel the essential power of the energy that dreams him/her. Also the dreamers meet the Earth body and learn how to relate to Earth energy through the human form. The dreamer reaches out to understand and learn from what has been dreamed.

Exercise 16. **Moving the Core Dreamer who dreams us**

To explain this very difficult idea, a movement exercise will help. This exercise is best done in the dark and with the eyes shut.

First, find a good connection of your feet with the floor, the Earth.

Be still and listen to the breath.

Gradually, allow your breath to move your body very gently from side to side. The movement of your body is then co-ordinating with the natural movement of your breath.

Take your attention gently to your hands. Gradually open to their movement. You do not have to direct the hands, they will move by themselves. It may be very simple and small movements; it may be larger and complex movements. The natural breath speaks through the body, and the hands begin to lead you.

Gradually open other parts of the body. The body will move by itself, without thought. The body does not need to be directed; rather it directs itself naturally from the energy of the breath. Be open to the body taking you to unusual positions that you have never been in before. Once you have overcome the obstacles of your conditional habitual movements in your body, your dreamer can begin to speak to you through the spontaneous intuitive knowing which is inside you. Something is moving you even though you are moving by yourself.

There is a sense in which there is a part of you that is projecting yourself onto this moment. It has the perspective of how you are connected to every other part of the universe. If you are connected to your dreamer, you move with fluidity and in harmony with all that is around you because your dreamer who dreams you is part of the great dreamers of the universe. You don't have to think. This is an exercise in connecting with the greatest part of your consciousness. It is exhilarating to discover that the body moves by its own accord and knows exactly where it wants to move and why. When you listen to your own dreamer who dreams you, there is no doubt; there is no need to question. The body moves because it moves, it dances to dance, like the universe. And that is that.

To connect with your own dreamer is not difficult. Openness. Trust in yourself, your own knowledge, and your own truth. Everything that is needed to be known is in your body at any moment. Now.

The varying vibrations of thought which reverberate through the whole universal dream including the thought vibrations of all planets and stars, can only be perceived – touched – by the human Earth body, if the information is transformed. The feeling of our emotions, the sight of colour, form, structure; the sounds, smells, sensations, are all the means by which the heart chakra translates the energy of the universal dream into the Earth body experience. Likewise, it is through the heart chakra that the energies of all other consciousness in the universe can hear and understand the Earth human experience. The human is one of the major channels through which the Earth is in direct communication with the planets, the stars, and all beings in the universe. In the human being are not only the Earth experience, but also the experience of the whole universal mind. There is nothing that is alien to a human. There are no aliens. 'Aliens' are only disconnected parts of the same self.

The breath is the magical tool through which this incredible two-way communication can be achieved. Use your in-breath to draw up the Earth energy through the base chakra, and breathe out through the heart chakra to the wider universal dream. The awareness of self expands. The dreaming body of the human Earth being opens out to dance in the universal breath of life.

Exercise 17. **Fifth Chakra Meditation**

The song of the whole dream is expressed through the fifth chakra, the throat.

Through this opening, the human body can breathe in the harmony of the universal song and can understand the sounds of all bodies in all spaces. The different vibrations of the dream can be felt through the resonance of each sound, be it word, or song, or hum, or sound without description. The word 'song' also describes the sounds we hear through colour and shape, the whisperings of our feelings, the sensing of our intuition. The song is the expression of the dream in all its forms.

The throat chakra is an opening. Breathe in the song of the universal dream, and breathe out through the heart chakra. The heart chakra is where the universal dream meets the human Earth body.

A strong meditation is to breathe in the universal song through the throat chakra and at the same time breath in the Earth energy at the base chakra. Breathe out their union at the heart chakra.

Exercise 18. **Sixth Chakra Meditation**

The dreaming body can see through the third eye on the temple chakra

The kind of seeing that is possible through the third eye is not only that of images. We can 'see' feelings, we can 'see' energy and we can 'see' time. It is through this seeing that we are able to develop the ability to move beyond the surface of appearances. We can perceive deeper into the fundamental truths of the information presented to us in the dream. When the sight is unified with the breath, there is no limit to the journeying in the great mind spaces of the universe.

If the attention is held at the third eye alone, the physical body can easily be forgotten. The other parts of the universal dream can seem very alluring and those with fluid vision can fly through great dreams of possibility. But we are here and now in physical form and the job is to connect the fluid dream to the comparatively fixed spaces of the physical. The dreaming body is the medium through which this is possible. The dreaming body is in the stars as well as the Earth, in the physical body as well as the energies of light and shape and emotion. For this reason, it is important to maintain awareness of the other chakras when breathing through the third eye. This may sound complicated, but as the attention of the dreaming expands, we are able to unify the attention of different aspects of ourselves. The dream is only fully conscious when we experience it through the whole of our body. It is possible to dream the elements, the trees, rocks, animals, the human teachers, colours, form, the planets, the stars, and all other conscious beings in the universal one mind through the magical open aware conscious human body.

First of all breathe in the sight of the dream through the sixth chakra and breathe out the meeting with the Earth body at the heart chakra. Then breathe up energy through the base chakra, opening the second, and third. At the same time, breathe down energy from the sixth chakra, opening also the fifth. Breathe out through the heart chakra. The dreaming body meets the physical body; spirit becomes matter through the magical medium of the breath.

Exercise 19. **Seventh Chakra Meditation**

The seventh chakra is our direct connection with the source, the energy even before the First Breath; energy without intention, unconditional love. It is the connection to the battery of the light body, which will charge and give spirit to the physical body.

When this chakra is open, each in-breath will draw in the energy of the greatest of spirits. The sensations of heat, of tingling, of lightness, of love without cause, of subtle and sustained orgasmic ecstasy, are all typical of the experiences of the human mind-body when it breathes its own spirit. For this energy to pass through the body, all the chakras have to be open to receive it, and the reward for the attention the mind gives to opening the chakras on the body is quite simple: bliss.

The jewels of the in-breath through the seventh chakra are needed by every chakra in our body.

Breathe in through the seventh chakra, breath out through the sixth, this will open the internal eyes.

Breathe in through the seventh chakra; breathe out through the fifth, this will help the flow of the song.

Breathe in through the seventh chakra, breathe out through the heart chakra. When the energy that comes through the seventh chakra meets the Earth body at the heart, it is like silver meeting gold. The cup of the gold Earth body drinks the silver offering. A huge meditation for the heart chakra is to breathe in from the base and from the crown at the same time, and to breathe out at the heart.

It is difficult for the lower chakras to directly receive the kind of vibrational energy that comes through the crown. In general, the heart is the receptor and translator of these energies. However, when you have been practising these meditations for some time, your energy body will be developed enough to open the lower chakras to receive the energy of the source.

Breathe in through the seventh chakra, breathe out through the third, this will help to dissolve our fear.

Breathe in through the seventh chakra, breathe out through the second, this will intensify and yet soften the seat of power through both the masculine and feminine principles.

Breathe in through the seventh chakra; breathe out through the base. This is like the silver journeying to the centre of the planet. The base chakra is the connection with the centre of the planet. When the Silver Spring touches the centre of the Earth, there is such a sense of deep hunger and thirst being met. It is as if for all these aeons, the lonely planet of Earth has been wandering through the universal desert looking for food and water. When the humans open the dreaming body completely to the energy of their source, the plight and search of the planets as well as the humans is over. There is no more hunger, no more thirst. There is only breath, the pure experience of the whole body, head to toe, planet to planet, star to star. The breath of the universal body.

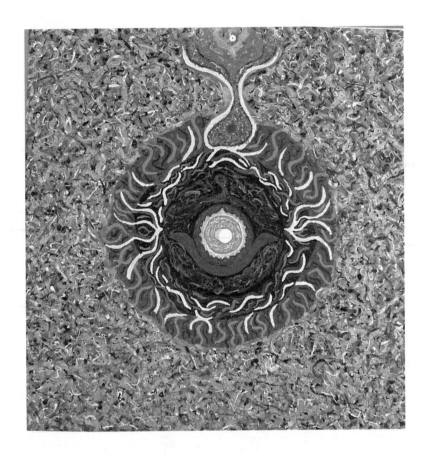

NINE - THE HEALERS
OF THE UNIVERSE

The human body reflects the universal body

The human body is more than it appears to be. It extends beyond its apparent boundaries and incorporates spaces and times beyond the place of our fixed attention in the material world. Planets and stars extend from the bones, limbs and organs of the body and conversely the body extends from planets and stars in the universe.

To heal the human body is to heal the Earth planetary body and to heal the universal body. They are all intricately interconnected. All is one and one is all. When we attend to our own health we are attending to the whole of creation.

The Soul Journey

Full consciousness is outside of thought and so outside the mind of the universe. The soul breathes from this enlightened place of no-thought, the place of all knowing. The soul comes from the place where there is no separation between itself and anything else. It is all. A soul is the soul. *Soul.* The word soul means essence. *Soul* is all one, connected to all that is, without any sense of difference. Once it enters the universal mind space it becomes separated, the individual soul within *Soul.* The individual soul is a separated dream within the whole universal dream. The root of your soul is the same as mind: we come from the place of completion.

If our soul came from the place of completion, why did it move into the separated and therefore less conscious place of the dream: why did your soul enter the universe? The answer lies in the concept of time. We come from completion, fullness of emptiness, the place beyond all duality and separation, and this is also where we are going. We are going back to where we have come from. The journey of the individual soul is a circle, like a breath. From full consciousness, to sub-consciousness, to full consciousness again. It is more a backward movement than a forward movement. It is the movement of memory. Our soul entered the universe in order to remember something.

Why? Why the need to remember?

The universe is a mind. The universe is a body. The universe is a mind-body. There is a type of blindness in the body of the universe. The blindness is thought in the mind-body that is not aware of why it exists and what it is supposed to do. The individual dreams are unaware of the other dreams in the whole. The thoughts go back on themselves, like circles of desire; they cling to the same pattern for want of anything else to cling to. They are frightened to move. They are stuck. They cannot see beyond their own repeated pattern. This is harmful to the body; it clogs up the body and makes it more difficult to move. The energy cannot flow freely. The individual soul travels from the place of enlightenment (Soul) into the universal body in order to open the circular thought to sight. Insight. It is like releasing a blood clot. It is a journey of healing. When the individual soul becomes conscious of itself - sees itself - inside the body, the habitual circles open into new spaces, new possibilities. The illusion of an individual dream dissolves, and the mind is released into the fluid movement of dreaming the dance. The universal body loves to dance; it is the joy of its life. The intention of the individual soul is to make the body lighter (light=sight) so that the dance can be more fluid.

Death: The transformation through the physical body

The Elemental Movement of the Soul

The movement from the place of *Soul* – Completion – into the universal mind-body is magical. Nothing becomes something; the non-material becomes material. In the dream of the Earth, the individual soul moves through the whole circle of the four elements and spirals into the crystal centre from whence it begins its journey back to source. It is a long breath within breaths.

When the individual soul is breathed into the Earth's atmosphere, it speaks first the language of Air. The element of Air is the mind space of the Earth dream. This connects with the mind spaces of other dreams in the universe. The Earth is a living breathing being within the breath. The Earth body breathes within *Soul. Breath.* Air is the lightest of the elements and the nearest in quality to the energy of *Soul.* Through Air there is a potential very fast link to spaces beyond the individual dream. It depends on the quality of the Air Space. If the Air Space of the Earth mind is clear, then energy can move with freedom to other spaces in the universe. If the Air is clogged with the fast chatter of half-finished thoughts, and uncompleted dreams, then it is more difficult to move.

The force of energy behind the movement from the non-material into the material world is Fire. Fire fuels the breath of the universal body. It has the power to move the energy of *Soul* through the Earth body. It has the power to move the individual soul through the human body.

The Earth is a body and the element of Earth is a container of the individual soul as it journeys through this planet. Its vibration is unimaginably slower than the completion of *Soul*. It is also a lot slower than many other parts of the universal body. All bodies have soul – human, animal, tree, rock, and plant. All Earth bodies are part of the whole Earth body. The planet Earth itself is a body transforming energy through its own breath. An Earth body is needed to carry the individual soul through the Earth dreaming space, and deliver it safely to a place where it can continue its journey. Death. The death of the body is a natural part of the Soul breath. The last breath in the Earth body is the beginning of the next journey.

The individual soul transforms back to Air through the element of transformation: Water. Water will take the energy that leaves the body and transform it eventually into Air. Water has an inter-dimensional quality that allows for the subtle movement between different levels of reality. It may take a body – for example rocks and bones – years or centuries to be released completely from themselves, but they will always need Water to complete the task.

This is the Earth elementary circle. Water returns to Air and the cycle continues. The energy is held in the planetary atmosphere by the force of the Earth's in-breath. The in-breath of the planet is strong enough to recover all the energy of the elemental circle as well as breath in new energy from Soul. Energy does not return to source through the elemental cycle of Air-Fire-Earth-Water. The soul moves to another part of the universal body through the fifth element - Crystal.

The element of crystal in the planet sets up the duality that keeps the elemental circle turning. This is part of the Law of Opposites, which states that for anything to exist, there must be its opposite. The elemental circle of the planet is clockwise and the crystal in the planet, acting as the antithesis, moves anti-clockwise. (If the elemental circle were anti-clockwise, crystal would turn clockwise). It is the crystal's anti-clockwise spin that keeps the clockwise elemental circle in motion. The crystal energy is like the small dots of the yin-yang side. The opposite is always the strength behind the projection.

Crystal holds the charge that keeps the elemental circle turning. To reach that charge, we have to pass through the elemental circle. The movement is then not so much a circle as a spiral. It is the journey to the centre of the Earth –

I could feel the ends of the breath and had the feeling I was nearing my destination. There, at the edge of this dream, four gold Buddhas were sitting around a white globe. The globe was like water, and fire. Fire in water.

The four Buddhas were sitting, waiting, receiving. All the forms of energy journey towards the centre and here the four Gold Buddhas received them. They were the great guardians of the white globe, which was our destination. We had all been breathed into the white crystal centre of the planet. I had been shown the journey of the soul. Here in the middle of the four Golden Buddhas was the great crystal centre of true death, of pure transformation.(From chapter 4).

The movement is through the dreaming body into the centre of the Earth. The dreaming body is not limited by the physical body and can move through all times and spaces. The journey is towards the crystal centre. From here, the Earth breathes out, but not into the same elemental circle. It breathes out into space, and the journey of the individual soul energy continues. Eventually, it returns to source. It takes back with it the energy and insight from what it has learnt through its breath in the universal body.

Chu-Ra

Where do these ideas come from? From Chu-Ra, mostly, a Toltec teacher with an Egyptian name. She is the most reliable guide I know. Of her name, she says –

"Toltecs are more than Mexico; Egyptians are more than Egypt, and you are more than England."

Her method was to sit me down and get me to look directly into her eyes. She would then ask me direct questions

"What is Soul?"

"What is God?"

"Who are you?"

I visited her many times when I was in Mexico, and through

being with her, I understood more than ever how the different teachings come together. When I answered her questions, I was not sure who was speaking — her, me, another of my teachers. I asked her about this and Chu-Ra said —

"It doesn't matter who says what. What matters is what you feel. You know if it is right. Use your heart — USE YOUR HEART!"

To her I offer the spirit of this book. She is the guide who speaks through her eyes directly from her soul, the soul. Soul.

"What is healing?"

"Letting go," was my immediate reply, without thinking. When she asked this question, I had been working with clients for over five years. With all of them, whether they had emotional, physical, or psychological difficulties, the root always seemed the same — holding. Something they were holding from the past, something unresolved, something they hadn't felt, emotions they were holding in their bodies and hearts and minds, which came out as injuries, anger, or confusion. For the individual soul to complete its journey it needs to be light —

"So how do you heal?" she replied.

"Letting go."

"How do you let go?"

The core question. With a lot of patience. Here, and in the following chapters, are some suggestions.

The Dreamer who Dreams you

What song will calm the violence,
What breath will heal the wound,
What action will free the bird,
What love will remember flight?

Violation, the root of pain, is the dreamers invading space. The more the dream is extended into illusion, the more there is separation, alienation, grief, and abandonment. Violence is part of the dream. The dream wills to continue, it wills to 'know', it wills to develop. This is part of the creative principle of destruction/creation. The song that calms the violence is the song that calms the dream, slows the evolving fire so much, there is only breath. In this breath is love. Innocence. There is a connection to a dreaming that becomes playing, dancing. From the other side of the stars that dream, from the Sun, from the creative fire itself, the breath lets go into flight.

What bird can fly so far; what bird has no need to land? In ecstasy, the body lets go of itself. The dreamer has no intention but to breathe, to love, just for this moment.

One breath. Lightness. An eternal kiss. There is unity.

Which dream dreams us? The family, education, culture, is only a small part of the dreamers that dream us. The land, the sky, the planets, the stars, are all dreamers. To reach the core dreamer is to reach pure thought, and this is the beginning of the ecstatic mystery. The individual soul dissolves into *Soul*. It is like passing through layers – family, culture, animals, trees, rocks, the elements, the planet Earth, the planets, the stars, the universe. Each layer of the dreamers' illusions can gently fall away. The traumatic dramas lose their grip. If we heal with care, they lighten. If we try and force it suddenly, with the cutting of the knife, it creates another dream of violence. A dying leaf hangs on the branch by a thread. It will fall when it is ready. To cut it would draw blood. In blood is revenge. The breath has its own timing to release. A true death cannot be rushed.

What is healing? Letting go into trust that love is there, that even though the baby falls, it will land softly; and falling into the arms of *The Mother* is like *The Father* falling into flight. The dream is no more than a dream. The child of the creative breath is no more than the breath.

Letting go

Go through every object in your possession. What do the objects remind you of? What kind of energy does the object hold? Every object holds energy, which can be connected to a particular person or a particular experience. Some of these associations may not be of your own life experience. Some objects hold the energies of other people and their memories, even other cultures and their memories. This is particularly true of objects like paintings or sculptures.

I remember going to someone's house to give a consultation, and the person had in their living room an African mask which was, for her, just something to remind her of her holiday. It held a very powerful energy and was dominating the room. The client told me she was having dreaming of African spirits entering and talking to her. This did not surprise me. I told her about the power of the object, and then it was up to her if she wanted to continue the dreaming connection with this object or not.

Another client has a room full of boxes. She said she wanted to clear the room, but all the objects reminded her of her late husband. Every time she tried to go through the papers and clothes, she would be overwhelmed with tears. Although this was difficult for her, going through the objects and letting go of them was part of her grieving process. In a sense, the room full of boxes was like her own mind, full of memories that dominated her space, and prevented her from being present. The objects, like her memories, were blocking the fluid movement of her life. She felt stuck.

All possessions influence the energy in the physical space and therefore also the mind space. Is the object useful? Is it needed? Does it weigh you down on your journey? Can you let go of this object with all its memories and associations? Can you give it away? Can you let go? The clearer your physical space, the clearer is your mental space.

Go through every relationship you have. Write a list of people in your life, particularly those (physically dead or alive) who excite a strong reaction in you. Take the first person on the list, and meditate on this person. Is this relationship helpful to you? Do you want to continue with this influence in your life? If the relationship helps, what would help the relationship to grow?

If the relationship blocks the fluid movement of the dance of your life, meditate on the relationship a little more. What kinds of associations are connected with this person? Do they remind you of anyone else? Do you have a similar pattern of relationships that extend back, or continued after this relationship started? Often the heavy energetic charge in a relationship is because of what has been carried from a similar relationship. Letting go of one person can mean also letting go of a whole series of similar relationships.

Breathe in the memory and the associated memory of this relationship. Breathe in the memory very deeply. As you breathe in, you may find other associated memories hidden in your body. When you can breathe in no more, breathe out and intend to let go of this relationship, cut the ties and release. This breath may be repeated several times for one relationship over a period of time until it feels released.

How congested is your life? What do you do that is necessary and what unnecessary? To fly, we need space. A simple life will create space. What could you let go of in your life that would give you the space to fly?

Past Life Memories

Past lives are very powerful memories that reflect our personality. They are very powerful dreams, which can be even stronger than those of our parents. To reach them requires a journey behind our past. They are difficult to see, and so it is difficult to be conscious of their very old (at times ancient) forces that are dreaming us. The first task is to identify a past life influence, then we begin to have some choice over how the dream continues.

The principle of a past life can be extended to this lifetime. We often re-create experiences which remind us of relationships or events in this lifetime which were key factors in how we have been dreamed. The following exercise can help us to remember 'lives' we have forgotten in this lifetime as well as former lives.

Exercise 20. **Identifying – Remembering – A Past Life**

The first step is to make a space in which you are very comfortable, and where you will not be disturbed for up to three hours. This process can bring up very deep feelings and sensations, and it may take time to absorb the information in your body. You may need some time just to sit and breathe before you connect again with other people.

This meditation can be done laying down or sitting down. There are advantages and disadvantages in both positions. Lying down is the most relaxed position for the body and it can help the body to open up more to the areas of experience that you are trying to access. However, there is always the risk of sleep and it can be difficult to maintain your attention. Sitting up, especially with a straight spine, will maintain your attention and focus, but it can be uncomfortable after some time. This process usually takes about an hour and a half to two hours. You can experiment, or try a combination of sitting and lying.

It may also be very helpful to do this meditation with a trusted friend who can read it very slowly for you, and take you through the various stages.

The first part of the meditation is to clear your mind by watching the breath. Thoughts will come and go, but if you try not to engage in them, after a while they will release. Sometimes this can take some patience. The aim of the first part of the meditation is to arrive at an awareness of this moment NOW in this place HERE.

When your mind is settled, take your attention to what has passed in your life during the past 24 hours. Give yourself enough time to register what your experience has been.

Then take your attention to what has passed in your life during the past week. Give yourself enough time to register what your experience has been.

Take your attention to what has passed in your life during the past month. Give yourself enough time to register what your experience has been.

Take your attention to what has passed in your life during the past six months. Give yourself enough time to register what your experience has been.

Take your attention to what has passed in your life during the past year. Give yourself enough time to register what your experience has been.

Take your attention to what has passed in your life during the past three years. Give yourself enough time to register what your experience has been.

Depending on your age, gradually regress through the periods of your life —

Adult. (As a guideline — ages 28 upwards.)
Young adult. (Ages 21 to 28).
Youth. (Ages 17 to 21).
Adolescence. (Ages 13 to 17).
Childhood. (Ages 5 to 13).
Infancy. (Ages 1 to 5).
Baby. (Ages one minute to one year.)
Give yourself enough time to register what your experience has been.
Take your attention to the moment of your birth.
Take yourself into the womb of your mother.
Breathe in the womb of your mother.

Allow yourself to leave planet Earth.
Allow yourself to float freely without any body in space or time.
Allow yourself to move into a different time in the past.
Return to planet Earth but not to the womb of your present mother.

See to which part of the world your attention is taken.

Allow yourself to be born again into this past life.

Watch as the life develops. Do not try to manipulate your dream. Allow the dream to simply show you as if you are watching a film. You will be taken into a memory of a part of your present mind. Give yourself enough time to explore the memory of this life.

Gradually release the memory and allow yourself to leave the planet again and move into space.

Return to the womb of your mother.

Return to your birth, with care.

Return to your infancy, your adolescence, youth, adulthood.

Return to the past year, the past month, the past week.

Return to yesterday.

Return to today.

Return through your breath to the HERE AND NOW.

Breathe.

This exercise is not easy and may take some time. You may find yourself lingering in past memories of this lifetime. This is fine. This exercise can be a means of accessing memories of this lifetime. Allow yourself all the time that you need.

When you have accessed the memory of a past life, meditate on how it affects your present personality. This life is a resolution of past influential dreams as well as present influential dreams.

When a past life has been identified, there is some choice as to how to work with it. It may be a dream that gives energy to your healing, and it may be a dream that is part of the wound. This is for you to decide. If the dream gives energy to your healing, how can you bring this dream more into your daily life? If the energy is part of the wound, it is very much like a trapped soul. The past life is looking to complete their dream through you, so that they can continue their journey back to Soul. The following meditation will help them to move. This meditation requires a lot of skill and may take some practise.

Exercise 21. **Return to Source Meditation**

Start with a breath awareness meditation. Then connect your own mind, as much as you can, with a sense of completeness that is felt in the First Breath. Try and find within yourself the peace of unconditional breath, breathing for no reason but the joy of breath. Let your thoughts and feelings fall away until you are sitting and breathing and nothing more.

Bring into your mind, the Sun. Imagine the Sun is nearly setting and it is low enough for you to see into it without burning your eyes. Breathe into the Sun.

Bring into your mind the past life with which you have connected. Open the memory of this life and connect it with the Sun. Very gently offer the Sun to the life. If and when the life is ready to move, breathe it gently into the Sun. This is not to be forced. It is like opening a prison door to one who has been imprisoned for life after life. Freedom can be very scary. All you can do is open the door. It may take many attempts. All you can do is open the door and eventually the prisoner will get curious. When the life is ready to move, breathe it gently into the Sun.

We can technically connect with every past life because our mind is able to open to the whole of the history of the dream. As you consciously open, your conscious mind space expands, and so it touches many more past lives and trapped souls. The more aware of this you become, the less attached the uncompleted dreams are to you. They pass through you with the breath. Some of the work with the crystal skull is to consciously attract trapped souls and past lives so that the mind space of the Earth is cleared. Then the energy is not blocked by the past and can move more freely.

Daydreams and Nightdreams.
Sleeping and Waking

Waking and sleeping are different states through which we experience the dream. We can think we are more conscious when we are awake than when we are asleep, but this is inaccurate. There may be all kinds of unconscious dreams that motivate our daily actions about which we have little or no awareness. The unconscious arises into consciousness through the dream all the time. When there is awareness of our dreams during sleep or when we are awake, we can see into hidden aspects of ourselves. The awareness of our sleeping dreams informs the awareness of our waking dreams, and the awareness of our waking dreams informs the awareness of our sleeping dreams.

Many dreams during sleep are concerned with thought processes or events in our lives that are uncompleted. If there is something we haven't finished, we do it during sleep. If there is an emotion that hasn't been felt, it will come out in the night often in exaggerated forms (fantasies or nightmares) which reflect the strength of our need to feel it. These dreams bring the past into the present because we are still holding the past in our bodies. Dreams during sleep can give a clear indication of what we are holding. The dream itself may be enough to release what we need to release. But it may be necessary to go back into a sleeping dream in order to prevent the experience coming up time and again. This often involves facing our fears.

Meditating on these dreams can help us to face the aspects of our lives that we simply need to experience. If a dream is remembered, it is possible to return to it by calming the mind first with the breath, and then gently taking the attention back into the memory of the dream. Consciously remembering a dream in this way is like returning to a place that was only fleetingly visited. By simply breathing in a remembered dream, it is possible to see and feel more clearly the reality of that dream.

These meditations can be difficult because the dreams are often taking us to shadow (unseen) aspects of ourselves, which we find difficult to look at. It can be enough during the meditation to feel consciously whatever it is we are supposed to feel, or to think whatever it is we are supposed to think. What is no longer needed, we can release with the out-breath. Often the dreams do not remain the same, and re-visiting the dream can begin the process of moving through into other dreams and memories, which explain the initial dream. In time, the dream moves and transforms. Nothing remains the same. When we truly let go, there is space for the dream to open.

Not all dreams during sleep are the working out of our personalities. When there is space in the mind, there is a possibility of communicating through the dreaming body to other beings in the Earth dream, or even other beings in the universal dream. This is the opening into the opposite, the anti-clockwise mentioned in Chapter three. We open up to energies closer to the source. The spirits of rocks, trees, plants and particularly animals can relate to us directly through our night dreaming. We may also communicate with other humans who are known to us or not known to us. Some people experience very unusual presences in their dreams such as beings of light or beings of colour, spirits that communicate to us when our minds are completely relaxed and open. When the mind is not held by the drama of the personality, there is a potential for clear telepathic communication.

Many dreams during sleep are mixtures and can relate to the personality as well as energy outside the personality. They can be a fast and surreal cocktail. When we consciously return to them, we can select what is useful to us. This is the same process as looking back over our activity during the day. Of all the various impressions and experiences of one day in the dream of our lives, there may be some scenes or moments which we highlight with our memory. There are strong symbols in the day as well as the night, waking or sleeping, and our conscious attitude to them can be the same – to bring them to our view so that we can see them more clearly.

The conscious dreamer can be aware that they are dreaming whilst sleeping. They can reach the same state during sleep as they can during their conscious dreaming of their practise. This can give them the ability to focus on particular aspects of the dream that interests them, and to make decisions that actively influences the whole dream. A conscious dream during sleep is a vibrant experience. All the different parts of the dream take on a quality that makes them more 'real', as if all the parts of the dream are charged with energy. It is at these moments that the conscious dreamer has more attention, and in truth, they are more awake than ever.

The conscious dreamer is also aware that they are dreaming whilst waking. Every part of the daily dream has the same energetic charge as the conscious dream during sleep. But because of our conditioning, and the way in which we take the daily dream for granted, our senses are often dulled. We tend to be unaware of the kind of energy that is part of our daily dream as if we are sleep walking in the dream of our day. The dreamer of the day can consciously realise the energy that charges the dream.

Attending to the sleeping dream helps to develop consciousness in our waking dream; and attending to our waking dream helps to develop consciousness in our sleeping dream. The practise of attending to the whole dream cuts through the illusions of the dreams we have been unconsciously following, and gives our movements and decisions a sense of deep authenticity. The whole of our being is connected and committed to the deepest sense of what we know to be real.

Conscious sleeping and waking dreams are an opportunity for dreamers to be at one with their own minds. The dreamed and the dreamer become one and there is a sense of the dream being co-created. The most advanced outcome of these experiences is the dreamer becoming aware in the dream that there is no difference between the dream and him or her self. When the division between subject and object dissolves completely, the dream opens up into fields of luminous energy, and the dreamer, ready to let go of all holding, dies into bliss.

Interpreting the Dream

The messages of the dream, waking or sleeping, can be mystifying. The experiences of dreams of night and day, conscious or half-conscious, can be approached in the same way. An analytical approach tends to be what we favour in our culture, but it can be premature. The intellect likes to analyse like the child likes to snatch. Some dreams cannot be held in such a neatly packaged definition. A more open intuitive approach is more accurate. The dream feels its way through us and the 'meaning' can take time to surface. I have had dreams during meditations and dreams during sleep that have taken years before I was in the space to receive them.

With patience in mind, there are some things we can do which can help us to clarify our experience. If there is a scene in the dream, it can be drawn or painted. The style of it doesn't matter; it is not an examination. It could be a diagram or a set of symbols, which helps to get a sense of a spatial perspective in the dream.

The dreams can be written down. The writing process can help us to see the dream more clearly.

If there is a place in the dream that is known, the place can be visited to see how the dream is trying to direct us. I have often followed dreams to places without knowing why. In fact, most of my travelling is the result of seeing places or receiving messages in night dreams. The answers soon come, perhaps through a feeling of déjà vu, perhaps through a feeling of inner knowing, a sensing that this is the right place to be right now.

The dream can be moved through the body. A dream may be so strong that it is felt in the bones. If the body is open to being moved by the dream, the body will move more consciously through the dream, and an incredible dialogue can begin between the physical body and the dreaming body.

The body moves the vision and the vision moves the body. When the internal life meets the external life, there is a full and complete experience.

There are dreams of sound. We can connect with the sound through our own voices. Singing, humming, chanting. The different vibrations can bring the dream more clearly into the body and the body into the dream.

A dream can always be returned to at any time for as many times as one likes. Then it is easier to focus on one aspect of the dream that needs attention. If there are animals, humans, or moving spirits in the dream, we can focus on them with our attention. In a conscious dream, there is interaction, and so a clear relation can be developed. In the case of animals and humans, it is particularly useful to hold the attention on the eyes. We can ask simply with our hearts open – "Who are you?" The answer may not come in words; it may come through the dream opening into another dream. Animals, humans and moving spirits are often teachers who want to show us something. If we can find the child in us who is humble enough to learn, we can receive our own wisdom through our own dreaming.

It may be enough to return to a dream that keeps speaking to you and simply be with it. Listening. If we are truly open to its energy, the dream will seep into consciousness, and like a powerful drink which is absorbed into the body, the soul will feed from it. Gradually, with openness and patience, we digest our own wisdom and move from the place of no doubt.

What is the meaning of a dream? It may mean that our body moves in a certain way, that we say something to someone, that we think something, that we feel something. The meaning of a dream is how it influences our consciousness and sometimes this cannot be measured, identified or classified. There are different levels of knowing. The kind of knowing a conscious dream holds is how the dreamer intends the soul through the universe. This is something only you can know, and it can be impossible to explain. Yet in one instant, it can be 'seen'.

Exercise 22. **Making a Ceremonial Space**

Conscious dreaming is a re-sensitising process. Our sensitivities have been dulled by years of abuse in contemporary society, particularly in the cities where everyone is a 'survivor'. The level of violence and indifference in our everyday lives and through the media means that we have to put up very strong boundaries just to stay standing, let alone functional. The conscious dreaming process is an opening re-sensitising process, and it can mean that big changes are made when we become aware of what we have put up with all these years! However, we still have to function, and for this, protection is necessary. Sacred ceremony provides the structure within which the dreamer can open into a space and then leave the space strong and able to meet whatever he or she has to meet. Ceremony creates a clear sense of when the conscious dreaming session begins and when it ends. This is really helpful, particularly at this advanced stage.

To set up a ceremonial circle is not difficult or time-consuming. First of all in your space, make a medicine wheel big enough for you to sit in and to move. In the four directions put symbolic objects that hold the energy of that element. Call in the elements, starting with the element of Air in the North, then Fire in the East, Earth in the South, and Water in the West. To 'call in' means to open up your heart and to your personal dreaming space to this spirit. It can be done with song, a musical instrument, or prayer –

"I call in the element of Air!"

Intention is more important than method. If your intent is clear, you can't go wrong.

When you have made your medicine wheel, smudge all the way around the wheel in a clockwise direction, as many times as you feel are right. Do the same with water, sprinkling as you go around the circle. More Fire smudge will accelerate the energy of the space; more Water will slow and calm. It depends on what you feel is needed as to what is the combination.

When you feel ready, you can begin your dreaming session in the centre.

When you have finished your session, thank the elements in turn, starting with the Water, and going anti-clockwise. Smudge and sprinkle with water, also anti-clockwise. As you are closing the circle, be aware of the transition from this sensitive space to the everyday space, particularly if you are going outside. Finally, massage your feet and stretch.

Sometimes, making a sacred space is not possible, and we are opened up anyway, particularly at night. Try and get up as slowly as you can. This will help you to remember your dreams also. A meditation to start the day, even before eating, can help to move from the night dreaming into the day dreaming space. This transition needs care and attention to avoid developing foul moods. This is a very sensitive time. Even nightmares will calm, given the right time and space. A bath, a cup of tea, swings in the hammock; whatever eases the body and mind into the next step of the dance. Nothing ever stays the same. The dream is always transforming.

If you find it is all getting a bit too much, go back a little to the basics. Sit with a tree. Meditate on a triangle on the second chakra. Above all, breathe. Breathe naturally.

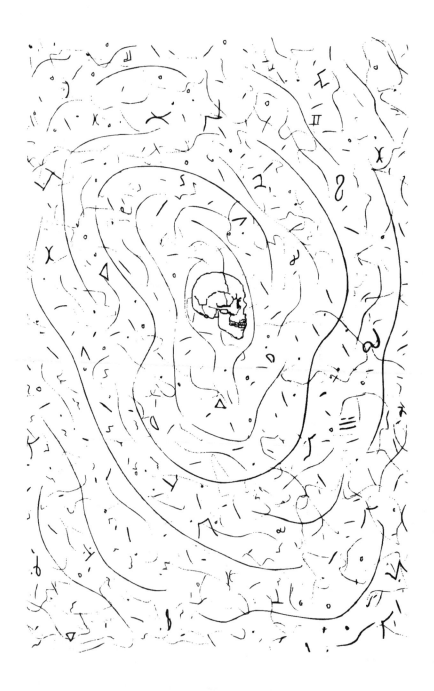

TEN - THE CRYSTAL SKULL

The Human Mind has the potential
to be Crystal Clear

I first heard about the crystal skulls during a course on North American Shamanism, which was held in North Wales. It was only mentioned in passing, and I didn't really think much of it. However during the next few months, it came up in my dreaming time and again, and so I decided to investigate further. I read some books of channelling from the skull, and about the few which had been found. I read about the Mitchel-Hedges skull, a beautiful skull found at Lubantuum, Belize, with an incredible healing energy, said to be Mayan; and I read about the Paris skull which was holding such negative energy, it led one of its keepers to kill himself. Scientists are not able to date or explain how some of the skulls have been made, so there is all kinds of speculation as to their derivation. Some say there were made by the Mayans, some by the Atlanteans; some say they are from Lemuria, some say from the Pleaides, and some say from Sirius. Whatever their derivation, they are objects of incredible power which attract a lot of attention. My investigation held my attention for a while, but then I became interested in something else, and apart from their appearance in a few night dreams here and there, I forgot about them.

The skull came back again most strongly in the Amazon jungle. I had been travelling with a Peruvian shaman for a while, and some of the ceremonies I did with him, together with the power of the jungle, seemed to open up my energy body to the point when the trees began to speak clearly. The trees spoke into my bones, they spoke into the depth of my body. As I heard them, I heard the voice of the crystal skull speaking from the planet. The trees were the medium of their communication.

It is impossible to say what was 'said' exactly, it is more a case of what was felt. It is like a wake-up call, as if the life had been like sleep walking, and suddenly, the body had a sense of purpose and direction without exactly knowing why. My body began to move with such strength, there was no need for reasons. It knew. A deep knowing, deeper than theories or explanations. If I stopped its movement whilst it was in connection with its knowing, there would be confusion, possibly even illness. It had known all along, and now it was saying – of course – I had to go to Mexico.

I had to go to Mexico. I hadn't even thought of Mexico, but because of visions and night dreams, certain books and conversations, the body had made up its mind very quickly. The mind I speak of in the body is not the same mind as the intellect. In fact the intellect is often denied control in these situations. The intellect helps in the making of the decision – it receives information in its mechanical way – but then it is left high and dry, like it thought it knew what it was dealing with, but now it slipped away like an invisible swallow. This is very frustrating for the intellectually inclined, but really these decisions cannot be held by the word and manipulated. So I knew I was going to Mexico, but I didn't know why. It was an act of faith. The reason would become clearer with time. Trust in what the body knows.

I often wonder why the dream is not easily related through the intellect. The dream doesn't really like the small spaces of explanations and theories. The energies of the dream can sweep through in great waves and the intellect prefers intricate buildings in which it believes it is safe. But if the wave comes then the wave comes, no matter how strong the building. And then there is breakdown.

Some people talk about the language of the heart. The feeling language of the heart. Perhaps the way the skull speaks is closer to that language. Something felt, but also something seen. The trees in the Amazon were like light. They felt like light and they looked like light. The language in which they spoke was that of light and colour. It is a different language to the language of words. It is bigger, less defined; it sweeps through in great waves. Like love. How can we really speak of love?

So the great wave from the crystal skull through the great trees of the Amazon swept me onto a plane to Mexico, and there I was in a state of forgetfulness.

So much of my journey has been about letting go of knowing and embracing mystery. Right down to the very next step. The wonder of a simple walk, of not knowing if I am going to go left or right. Every moment becomes a great adventure, and the senses are sharpened, we are listening - where to, where to now? I wandered through Mexico like this, not quite knowing why or where, but moving all the same, and enjoying the dance, a dance of forgetfulness, the dance of now, of just being with the energy that was around me. The dance took me to a place called Chetumal on the border with Belize, and there I wandered into the Museum of the Maya. I saw a Mayan priest figure who was called the Keeper of the Crystal Skull. It was like another wake-up call. Or course, I was going to Lubantuum in Belize, where the most famous of the crystal skulls had been found.

It is crazy, the idea that you can hold this energy; that somewhere there is an object in which the energy of the crystal skull is held. It doesn't seem possible that an energy so big could be held in something so small. But crystal skulls are tangible objects. They are quite simply skulls carved from quartz crystal. You can hold one in your hand and look into it, and then it looks into you. And the great wave of energy makes nonsense of its size and shape.

I don't quite know what I expected to find at Lubantuum. The crystal skull was discovered in the Mayan ruins, it has been said, in 1921 by Anne Mitchel-Hedges who is now its 'owner'. But there are lots of other stories. Some say it was taken from another island off Honduras. Some say the Mayans had a secret hiding place from which it was stolen. The ruins themselves are largely covered with the jungle growth of time, and so is the truth of the skull's origin I suspect. I realised that I had come to Lubantuum to discover that there was no reason to come to Lubantuum. The skull was speaking to me in its energetic way so there was no reason to hold the physical object. It was more inside of me than in a crystal object. It was breathing through me, in me. I came to Lubantuum to discover that there was no need to go in search of something that wasn't really a thing; there was no point in looking for something that was already me. I might as well look in the mirror.

This left me with a question - what is the point of the form? Does the energy come from some kind of holographic projection? At that time, I had only seen the crystal skull in the British museum, but the kind of energy I was feeling came from inside me. I was travelling a long way from the British museum and any physical crystal skull that I was aware of, yet the wave could hit me at any moment – in a train, in a plane – it wasn't limited to time or place – it would just sweep through when my mind was open to it, sometimes when I was doing the most inane things, eating a meal, going for a walk – whoosh – gasp. My body would feel sudden heat; I would stop whatever I was doing. My whole way of seeing that moment would change.

So what is the point of the form? Crystal and skull. We know that crystal stone holds a very high frequency of energy; that crystal is used for healing all over the world by many tribes and different traditions. It has the power of amplification and clarification. It can move energy and direct and clean or clear blocked energy. The skull is traditionally the place of mind. The seat of the mind. Not just the intellect, but of the mind. The mind that is bigger than the body. The mind that is the doorway to the infinite. The Buddhists, great scientists of the mind, say you cannot see the mind or hold the mind. Some of the Buddhists even say that the mind does not exist. But popular imagination has it that the mind is in the skull. Like an icon for the digestion of our limited intellect. So what is the crystal skull? Amplified mind, clarified mind. Or, from a Buddhist perspective, amplified nothingness!

Whoosh. It is easier to feel it than to explain it.

Looking into pure nothing is scarier than anything else I have known. It is a complete insult. It insults my being. It insults my existence. I become less significant than an ant, and all (and I mean all) my passions and great concerns seem at best irrelevant and at worst ridiculous. I can barely breathe; I don't know how to breathe in the face of space beyond space and time beyond time. It is outside the language of my body, which knows limitation, form, time, place and a sense of progression. The way I describe it probably sounds nihilistic, self-defeating perhaps, death-like even; yet learning to breath into the huge mystery is like learning to live. It is the purest paradox I know. In nothing – in no time, in no space, with no context and no shape or form – there is the greatest energy, and just to breathe in it becomes a life's work.

The crystal skull, icon of the expanding human consciousness, is the doorway to what the Mahayana (Tibetan) Buddhists call the luminous mind. After the lessons of Lubantuum, I gradually realised that my work was to learn how to be in the energy of the skull on a more sustained level. So rather than waiting for its energy to appear at any moment, I began to call it up, simply by visualising, and tried to breathe through my experience without fear of hyperventilating or burning up or just going mad. It wasn't easy, and I quite often deliberately tried to block it out. But it was leading me, I knew that much. Whether I was conscious of its energy or not didn't seem to matter – it would lead me!

For a year or so I carried on like this, only daring to look it in the eye occasionally, but knowing I was looking at it even without my conscious eyes. It moved me around the world, and I had various experiences and met various people. It was like, I suppose, some kind of waiting game. Waiting until the time when I would be able to see it directly. I am only saying this in retrospect. All I really knew was that I was being led, but I didn't really know why or where. I was looking at life in a state of wonder, and I was taken, like a puppet on a string, here and there, letting go of my will, and finding, on being led, the beauty in the smallest things. A piece of drift wood on a beach. The way the man carries the basket of rocks. The way the woman talks, a leaf that falls. And walking by seas and through jungles and over mountains and into deserts, I found myself in Mexico again, in the desert, and I was being taught by a human and the spirit of a cactus, how to listen to the rocks.

The stars speak, in sound and light. Lying on the desert floor, they speak in whispers, as if they are very near, as if they are all around us. The rocks come from the stars, and they speak as if they are my bones, as if there is no difference between my body and the Earth and the Earth and the Stars. They speak directly with a light that blinds.

This is the source. In the night sky of the mind, an energy comes into the head, and takes over the body, directs the breath, needs the breath to direct it into the body, around the body; needs the breath to direct it into the Earth. As the energy from the stars reaches through all the chakras of the human body, it reaches also the centre of the planet. And there, in the centre of the planet, the skull can be seen, can be felt, and the light that is pumped like blood around the body, is reflected from the skull into a thousand colours. The mind ceases to be the body; and the body ceases to be the mind. There is a moment of incredible blindness as we are taken into the memory of our connection with our ancestors.

The body becomes an energy far greater; the planet becomes an energy far greater than its form. During the moments when the starlight meets the skull, the illusions are dispelled and there is great change. Something moves in the consciousness of humanity. Something moves beyond the circle of the human understanding of time. There is the possibility of evolution. There is the possibility of progress beyond habitual patterns. There is choice. If the heart is open . . . . .

Exercise 23. **The Inner Crystal Skull Meditation**

The crystal skull is an energy that is inside all of us. There are quartz crystal skulls that have their own power, but the physical object is not necessary to access the energy. Working with the inner crystal skull is not to be taken lightly. This is a very powerful energy. As a guideline, the whole of the programme in this book is designed for at least a period of two years. You are advised to work for at least a year and a half on techniques in the preceding chapters before attempting to connect with this energy. However, with this caution in mind, here is the information I can offer you.

This meditation is in three parts. Each part should be practised for one month regularly before continuing onto the next part.

Part One

First of all, a very quiet and undisturbed ceremonial space is essential. This is serious work. Make sure you have at least a day in which you can begin to digest the energy with which you connect.

Set up your ceremonial space and medicine wheel as suggested in the previous chapter.

Start with the breath awareness meditation.

After about fifteen minutes, take your attention to the heart chakra. Maintain the awareness of the natural breath.

In this exercise, you can find your own sense of timing. I will describe the steps, but so much of this technique is in the timing, which only you can discover for yourself. When the timing feels right, take your attention to the front of the head.

Take your attention to the right side of the head.

Take your attention to the back of the head.

Take your attention to the left side of the head.

Take your attention to the top of the head.

Repeat the attentions to the five areas of the head.

Feel your own timing. Maintain awareness of the natural breath, your heart chakra opening.

Repeat the attentions to the five areas of the head a third time.

With the heart chakra open, take your attention upward and outward towards your sense of stellar energy. Open your heart and mind to this energy. With each out-breath, take your attention further towards and into this energy. Some people feel this energy very close to them and do not feel the need to journey very far outwards, others prefer to journey into the sky to touch the stellar energy. It helps to try and see the energy as light.

When you feel you have arrived, breathe into this energy.

When you are ready, breathe the energy towards the top of the head.

With your in-breath, draw in the energy into the top of the

head, and with your out-breath breathe the energy down the right side of your head to the right shoulder.

With your in-breath, draw in the energy into the top of the head, and with your out-breath breathe the energy down the left side of the head to the left shoulder.

With your in-breath, draw in the energy into the top of the head, and with your out-breath breathe the energy down the back of your head to where the skull meets the spine (the pineal gland). With your in-breath, draw in the energy into the top of the head, and with your out-breath breathe the energy down the front of the head as far as the neck.

With your in-breath, draw in the energy into the top of the head, and with your out-breath breathe the energy down the whole of the head as far as the neck and shoulders.

This is called the upper triangle.

With your in-breath, draw in the energy as far as the shoulders, and with your out-breathe breathe the energy down the arms as far as the hands.

See if you can feel the energy collecting in your hands.

With your in-breath, draw in the energy to the point where the skull meets the spine, and with your out-breath, breathe the energy down the whole of the spine. Take your time to feel all the parts of the spine.

With your in-breath, draw in the energy as far as the bottom of the spine, and with your out-breath, breathe the energy down through the legs, as far as the feet.

See if you can feel the energy collecting in your feet.

With your in-breath, draw in the energy as far as the throat area, and with your out-breath, move the energy down through your chest, your stomach, as far as the base chakra.

Focus your attention on the base chakra.

Focus your attention on the crown chakra.

Feel the relation between the base chakra and the crown chakra.

Breathe your natural breath.

When you are ready, open your eyes.

This is the end of the first part of the meditation. It would help now to massage your feet, and also to find a tree under which you can sit for a while.

Part Two

The second part of the meditation starts with an exact repeat of part one. The only difference is that after practising, you may find it easier to feel and move the energy, so it will not take as long. In this second part, a double pyramid is mentally drawn above and below the body so that the body sits inside the double pyramid.

Take your attention to a point above your head. With your out-breath, breathe a line, a corner of the pyramid in front of you.

Take your attention to a point above your head. Breathe a line, a corner of the pyramid behind you.

Take your attention to a point above your head. Breathe a line, a corner of the pyramid on your right side.

Take your attention to a point above your head. Breathe a line, a corner of the pyramid on your left side.

Draw the base lines, which connect the four corners of the pyramid.

Sit in the pyramid. Breathing your natural breath.

Begin to draw the upside down pyramid. From each corner

of the pyramid draw the lines going downwards, one by one, using your out-breath. Align the tip of the upside down pyramid with the upright pyramid.

Breath inside the double pyramid.

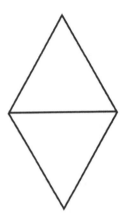

This is the end of the second part. Massage your feet. Return to the tree. Breathe with the tree.

Part Three

Stage three starts with a repeat of stages one and two. By now you should be fluid in the earlier meditations.

Remembering the energy of the stars, breathe the energy with the in-breath through the centre of the double pyramid. With the out-breath, breathe the energy down deep into the Earth. Stay with the movement of the energy of light and as much as you can, do not divert your attention from it. You are breathing down into the centre of the Earth. This will take as long as it takes. It may be that you need to do the meditation several times before you know what it means to arrive in the centre.

When you are in the centre, call with your attention to the crystal skull. You do not need to try very hard, just gently open. The energy comes to you.

Breathe in the energy of the skull.

Look into its eyes.

Stay just long enough to feel the connection. Do not linger.

With your in-breath, draw up the energy of the skull to the tip of the upside down pyramid.

In your own time, draw up the energy of the skull with your in-breath to the base point.

Gradually drawing the energy of the skull through your chakra points and your body up to the neck.

Pause with your breath.

When you are ready, breathe in the energy of the crystal skull into your own head. VERY GENTLY. Breathe the crystal skull into your own skull.

When the timing is right, give with your out-breath, the whole of this energy back to the star. DO NOT HOLD THIS ENERGY. GIVE IT BACK COMPLETELY. LET GO. RELEASE. **DO NOT HOLD.**

The energy is released.

Return to the consciousness of your breath. Your natural breath.

When you are ready, open your eyes.

Massage your feet. Do not move from your ceremonial space. Stay for as long as you can. Give your body enough time and space to breathe this energy.

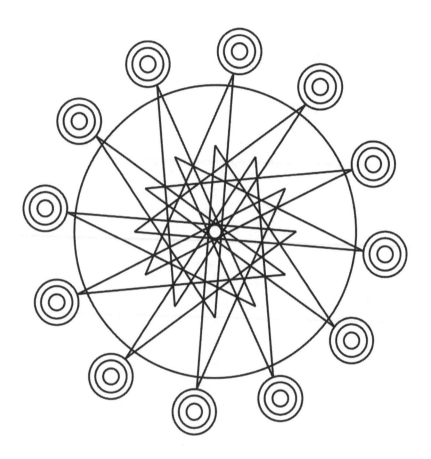

ELEVEN - THE CIRCLE OF 12

The history of the evolution of man is essentially the gradual awakening of the human Earth body to its own dreamer. All religions were stylised forms of the same intention – to connect with the (God/Goddess) designer consciousness in the rest of the universe. Because there are crystal skulls in all of the planets in our solar system, astrological understanding was a hugely important part of this re-connection. There was a point in the development of human consciousness at the time of the ancient Egyptian and earlier cultures of Mexico in particular, when the crystal skull connections between the planets were an integrated part of the spiritual life. Important decisions would be made in accordance with the balancing of the 13 planetary centres of the solar system. This balanced ring of 12 around the central sun allowed the consciousness of humanity to open to other areas of the universe where the designer consciousness is planted in other planets, and where the designer consciousness is still an observer and closer to the original breath.

The human mind was so open at this time that it was possible for the objective designer consciousness to feed the crystal skull seeds directly using the humans as mediums. This gave certain humans great power, which was at times abused. It was also possible for the design consciousness to cross-fertilise its ideas that had developed from one planet to another. Again the crystal skull was a powerful enough medium to affect this transition. This movement of energy would again, in human mythology, be an alien landing, but really it was just a connection of one part of the universal one mind to another part. Different planets and star systems in the universe have different aspects of experience, and the dreamers seek a union and interconnection of this experience. It is difficult for a planet to understand its connection with other parts of the whole when it can only see itself in its own context.

The crystal skull expands. Crystal grows. Crystalline consciousness will always seek to unify. After connecting with the crystal skull in the Earth, the dreaming body can expand to experience other planets. There are 12 main planetary centres in the solar system and one star, the Sun. The mythology of the crystal skulls is connected to the number 13. It is said by some North American and Mexican tribes that the gathering of the 13 skulls would be like the gathering of the ancestors to discuss the future of this planet. The Australian Aboriginals talk of the alignment of the 13. This alignment occurs when the Earth's axis shifts to a particular angle. The 13 skulls are connected to the 12 planets with the Sun making the 13th in the centre. When the planets in the solar system are aligned in the human mind, the dreaming body is prepared for a major shift in which it can begin to understand stellar energy.

This is also a major healing process. As the healing body expands, the physical body has to let go of all the emotional debris it is holding in the body. It is flight, and to fly we must be light. The more the mind opens to the crystalline consciousness, the more will be released. This healing process can be painful, at first, like Shiatsu, Acupuncture, or Deep Tissue Massage. The emotional toxins, increasingly powerful the deeper they are held in the body, are released. The death of parts of ourselves brings the possibility of life in another. The feeling of connection as the self expands is breathtaking. As the fears are released, the heart gradually opens to the love in the natural breath of the universe.

Exercise 24. **Connecting with Planetary Energies**

This exercise starts from the place of the crystal skull in the centre of the Earth. Once the energy has been touched using the exercises in the previous chapter, the attention of the crystalline consciousness can be directed towards the planets.

When you have connected with the skull in the centre of the Earth, intend with your out-breath your energy towards a planet. Use your out-breath to take your dreaming body to the planet. Breathe into the experience of this planet. Using your out-breath, breathe your dreaming body deeper into the centre. At the centre of each planet in the solar system is a crystal skull. It may take several journeys to the same planet in order to feel this. After each journey to each planet, use your in-breath to return to planet Earth. Return to the skull in the centre of the Earth planet. Connect the skull of the planet you have visited to the skull in the Earth. Breathe in this combined energy towards your base point and then up through the whole of your body. As the energy of the planet moves through your body, it will be grounded into your daily experience. When it has reached your head, let it go like you did with the Earth skull. This letting go process in effect creates a fluid channel between your energy body and the energy body of the planet. Complete the meditation with breath awareness.

Some people like to be guided to get a sense of what to look for, and some people prefer to go with a completely open mind. Depending on your propensity, it may be advisable to read the following after your journeying rather than before.

The following description of the journey through the circle of 12 planetary centres, is the journey of the conscious dreamer gradually opening up to the huge possibilities of the universe.

The Moon

There are 13 lunar months in one solar year and this is part of the ancient calendars, for example the Mayan and Celtic calendars. The Moon of 13 holds the Earth within its present time zone. The circles of time are necessary to hold the Dream of the Earth. The dream requires two essential properties to maintain itself: time, and space. The Moon holds the timing of the Earth dream. Circles of time hold the dream in the fixed attention. The fixed attention is what gives the Earth its material stability. Without the Moon, the Earth would not be able to maintain its form, and life as we know it, would not continue.

Connecting with lunar energy will help you to understand time. Many women in tribal cultures are connected to the lunar cycle by their own menstrual cycle. Each Moon has a particular quality. In the Celtic tradition, each Moon is connected to a tree, and the seasons were understood through the characters of the Moons.

The Moon is also the mirror of the Earth's self-reflection. The Earth sees itself through the mirror, which the Moon presents. The Moon is like the Earth's own camera. The Earth needs the Moon to have a sense of self. It is the Earth's primary relation: lover, mother, father, brother, sister, friend. The Earth understands itself through these mirrors and the Moon holds the possibility of all the significant others. In a sense, the Moon is transparent and is the means through which all the other energies of the planets in the solar system are presented to the Earth body. The Moon is the translator, because of its transparency, of the energies that are too distant and too fast to understand.

Through the Moon the dreaming body of the human can travel around the globe. The Moon draws dream lines in space with which the dreaming body can connect. It is possible for the dreaming body to be in any place on the Earth's surface through the medium of the dream lines drawn by the Moon. It is the same principle as the satellite that receives messages from one place in the Earth and transmits the information to another place. Electronic mail is possible because of this.

The dreaming body is not limited to one place and can be in many different places at the same time. For us to be aware of two places is an achievement, and this awareness is possible particularly through night dreams. Whilst the physical body sleeps, the dreaming body travels, often to places on the Earth that the physical body has not visited before.

The Moon will also help you to dream with consciousness at night. It is the strongest influence on the ability of our dreaming body to fly. The Unicorn and the Quelacorn (flying Unicorn) will help you to understand this connection. The Moon will give you the clarity of self-reflection you need to see yourself, to see how you dream; to see how you are being dreamed.

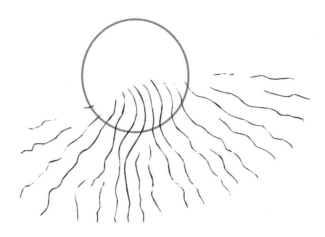

Exercise 25. **Ceremony at Full Moon**

The Moon, like rocks, trees, animals and humans, is a teacher of the dream. To open to the teacher's energy, here is a simple ceremony you can do at full Moon when the energy of the Moon teacher is strongest.

Get a black wooden bowl. It is best but not essential if it is African. Fill the bowl with clear quartz crystals. Take the bowl, a cup of water, a candle or wood for a fire, and incense to a high place. Make an altar on the hill. If there is no hill anywhere near you, at least be outside. Make a prayer to the Moon that it will help you to understand yourself, to understand your dreams, to learn to be conscious of your dreaming. Cover the crystals in water (natural not treated). Hold the bowl of crystals to the Moon as if you are giving them to your lover. When you have finished your prayer, place the bowl on the Earth. Take one crystal from the bowl, and place it in the Earth. Repeat this for every Moon in the calendar year. The Celtic lunar year begins in November at the start of winter. The Mayan lunar year begins in July.

Exercise 26. **The Mirror of Self-Reflection**

To move past the Moon to the other planets, we have to pass through the Mirror of Self-Reflection. To do this requires great courage because you will be moving into areas that are beyond your daily experience. To face your own mirror requires impeccable honesty. You will be facing who you really think you are.

First of all, write down a list of all the people to whom you have a reaction, physically alive or dead, either positive or negative. This can be anyone from your Mother to the person who sells you vegetables.

Start with a breath awareness meditation. Bring the first person on the list to your mind's eye. Look them in the eye. What part of yourself can you see? Breathe through your reactions of attraction or repulsion until you maintain with this person a steady gaze and you are simply breathing naturally. It is like waiting for ripples to calm after a stone has been thrown into the pond. The reactions of attraction and repulsion are natural ripples. The longer you hold the person's eye, the more time there is for the ripples to calm, and there is no more than still and silent water between you.

Go through the whole list. Bring up everyone who is currently moving your image of yourself. Only when ALL the images are calm can you pass through your mirror. This may take a lot of practise and patience and time. But at the end, for sure, you will understand yourself more than you have ever done before.

The Shadow

Behind the mirror is the shadow. The Moon holds the shadow of the Earth. It holds what is unseen as well as what is seen. The shadows are the parts of yourselves you deny or are not aware of. There are times when the Moon receives no Sun because the Earth is between itself and the Sun. There are times when the parts of the Moon are in the full glare of the Sun. The light and the shadow make a dance, which the Moon can teach you. The violence, fantasies, repressed desires, horrors of your shadows, are made easier to bare through the dance. Nothing stays the same. Light to shadow, shadow to light. The way through the back of the mirror is to accept and look the shadow figures in the eyes as you have done the people you know. Angels or devils, we have to pass through all. If you react to the dark and say you only want to be in the light; if you deny the difficult emotions, they will only grow and become even more monstrous than they already appear to be. Passing through the shadow is part of understanding who we are. Your desire to kill maybe as real as your desire to give birth; your desire to love as real as your desire to hate. This is a tough aspect of the conscious dreamer's journey. We have to face our fears. Our fears become monsters, devils, and demons in our dreaming if they are not faced. Do not run away – they are all aspects of your mind; they are all parts of your dream. When you become conscious of them, they will have less power over you.

When the shadows are exposed, they are no longer shadows. As we journey towards the star, there will be more shadows exposed, hidden aspects of yourself that can no longer be ignored. By facing them, they are exposed to your own light. They can no longer control you from behind.

It may seem at times that you just can't go on; that consciousness just isn't worth the struggle. Just when you think you've dealt with one demon, another one comes along. These dark nights of the soul can kill the will of the warrior, but if you get through them, there is incredible reward. Once the fears have been faced, there is so much less that can hurt you. You are stronger, surer of yourself. You move towards the place where there is no doubt, a deep deep authenticity. You know who you are.

Venus

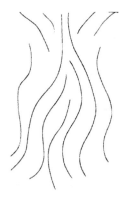

Venus is the centre where the passion can expand. Incredible sex, the most delicious meal, finest views, exquisite music, an incredible massage, and fine aromas. The pleasures move through their imagined path, and then even further. The Tiger is the guide into the centre of the heart's desire. When all the passions have been met, when all the things we thought we wanted are ours, what next? What happens after satisfaction? What happens when there is no longer hunger? Venus can take us to that place. Beyond hunger. This can be scary because almost all our attentions are on chasing after what we believe we want. Venus is the perfect seducer, but after we have consumed our desires, there can be a void and a sense of being lost. The question arises – What do I want? What do I really want? Venus will take you even deeper into your desire.

Coming back down to Earth can be bumpy. This is true in general as the dreaming body expands. The senses are fine-tuned and this means there is less resistance to things like traffic noise. The trick is to absorb rather than react. Our tendency is to react to what we don't like, and to be attracted to what we like. If everything is absorbed and accepted, there isn't this tension. Easier said than done, but there is a way in which Venus can come to Earth and be integrated even into the High Street.

If you are living the reality of Venus, unpleasant realities like traffic noise can take you away from that reality because it can seem at odds with it. But there are many parallel realities. Venus exists at the same time as the Earth. Love exists at the same time as suffering. Because there is suffering doesn't mean that love doesn't exist. Because there is noise outside doesn't mean there can't be peace inside. Eventually, suffering becomes part of love and noise becomes part of peace. As the dreaming body expands, more and more energy passes through. We become bigger than we thought possible. The self expands and absorbs all experience, and lets it all pass through with each breath.

Mercury and Merlin

The self expands as near to the Sun as it dares. Mercury will not consume you if you are bold enough to face its power. It is the power of Merlin.

Merlin enters through Uranus and activates from Mercury. I have known this for some years, but I had never understood it. Merlin for most of my life has been too enigmatic for me to describe. He takes on many forms, and came to me strongest as Confucius. I had never seen him as particularly Celtic.

All this changed in Glastonbury. I was leading a dreaming circle. The dreaming through the drum took me to many rabbits. They were dead and their souls were lifting off the bodies. They were following me. I seemed to be going towards an Oak tree. The rabbits entered into the open trunk of the tree, and began to descend. (The Oak tree is a classic doorway to the underworld.) I could see they were starting their passage to the centre. I began to feel anxious, tense. Some heavy energies entered my body and I felt something that has the power to manipulate energy. I seemed to be fighting a power that wanted to be in me. I didn't want to be that power and I didn't want to manipulate. I was saying no. Yet the energy was insistent. I saw all the authority figures and institutions, against which I had rebelled – family, church, university, government. My deepest anger was that humans were always taking power and using it to control others. I didn't want to be part of this. I wanted to stop drumming and to stop the session because I believed this energy was not helpful for the group or myself. But the energy wouldn't let me go. There was something in me that kept me moving deeper into it. I felt like I needed to arm myself with something and all I had was a drum and my song.

He appeared suddenly, in the traditional wizard form of the Celts. He was clear and crisp and staring at me. This was the biggest challenge of my life. Thank the song for helping me through it. This energy, this Merlin is directing stellar energy. He has the power to receive the direct light from the heat of the Sun and direct the energy to other stars and planets. His wand is phenomenal. I have never trusted this kind of male energy, always feeling that this kind of magic was very ego centred. But to know Mercury is to know Merlin. I was teaching about how to connect with the planetary energies and here was the lesson in my face. Teacher and pupil, if I wanted to progress, I had to take the staff and the wand. This is the challenge of Mercury. Through Mercury, the Sun is transmuted and the energy is sent directly to the crystal core of the other planets. I was meeting Merlin deep down in the heat of the Earth; he can live in fire. He lives like the burning bush that never dies.

Mercury is the power of the magician, the winged messenger who transmits energy from star to star, planet to planet. We have to pass through our deepest desires in Venus to reach this place. Mercury is not something desirable as much as something to be passed through on the road to consciousness. Mercury challenges directly our fear of power. Merlin's trick is to allow power to enter his being without holding it. It goes as soon as it comes. There is no need to hold the power because there is an infinite supply. Like the philosopher's stone or the Ring of Power in J.R. Tolkiens tales, power corrupts the one who tries to possess it. Merlin directs power like the dancer directs energy through the body. The continuous movement keeps the energy fluid, and it never has a chance to institutionalise into the abuse of authority.

There is also something else about Merlin. Time. He defeats it. He doesn't obey these laws. The universe is not linear and neither is he. Through Mercury it is possible to pass into timelessness. But not yet. Merlin can go into and out of time zones. You may pass out and not know how to re-enter. Better to follow the energy of the Sun. It will force you out; you cannot get any closer yet. It is a phenomenal effort to maintain the dreaming vibration of Mercury. Let go and the Sun will move you way out beyond the Earth, to Mars.

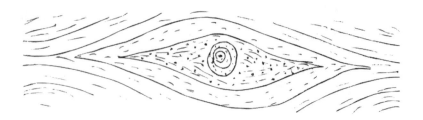

Mars

Mars is also a masculine principle of projection, but it doesn't have the wisdom of Mercury. The energy of Mars fights without quite knowing why. The heart is brave and the intent is to succeed and win, but what success is and what is to be won is unclear. A man can fight simply because he is a man — because that is what men are supposed to do! Yet this kind of blind faith on the journey can be needed when the going gets tough. When there is a long way to go, and everything seems useless and senseless, the energy of Mars will save you. It just keeps going because it keeps going. Onwards!

The Asteroids

Mars is tempered by the Asteroids - Juno, Aphrodite, Palleus-athene, and Vespa. In this part of the solar system, the masculine and feminine principles combine and it is here that the marriages between the opposite sexes and also the principles within oneself are played out. The male adventurer is balanced by the feminine love of the beauty in the moment. Timing now becomes crucial. Whether to go, whether to stay. There is a slowing down of the male projection from Mercury and Mars, it is time to reflect. Whether to party or to work, to change house and career or consolidate. The hero will only succeed if he understands the right time to wait and be. Enjoy. The heroine will blossom when she is not afraid to move with the motion of the energy that passes through the body. In the journey, this is the stage of waiting and learning before it is time to continue. If the hero passes through, and if the heroine always stays in the house, they will both die of an empty heart.

The Masculine and the Feminine

What is masculine?

What is feminine?

In your own terms, how masculine are you; how feminine are you. If you have a partner, how masculine is he/she; how feminine is he/she? In your relationship, homosexual or heterosexual, do you take on a particular masculine or feminine role?

Which motivates you more, the masculine or the feminine? If you have a strong tendency towards the masculine, how can you develop your feminine aspect (without projecting it onto your partner!)? If you have a strong tendency towards the feminine, how can you develop your masculine side (without projecting it onto your partner!)? To move further on this journey through the planets, the masculine and feminine sides need to find balance. This will balance the dreaming body and you will no longer react to something because of your physical sex and your internal sexual identity. Experience ceases to be limited to this duality. This will considerably free your mind.

Jupiter

Jupiter is the biggest planet in the solar system and for this reason it is misunderstood. The great figures of Jupiter and Zeus with the thunderbolt in Roman and Greek mythology paint an imposing and frightening portrait of this planet. But size is not everything. Jupiter is also the lightest planet in the solar system. One can lose oneself in the complex subtle layers of Jupiter. Entering Jupiter is like entering a balloon. It is full of apparitions, places that could be somewhere or nowhere. It is so easy to float through it and effortlessly fly through one of its billions of coloured channels. Does any of it lead anywhere?

What a phenomenal cavern of light! There is life here, consciousness. All the columns and lines and structures have a regulating function, which can only be made by minds who understand how to control such vast expanses of energy. Perhaps they don't need form. Perhaps what I see is their form. It is a very sophisticated technology and it regulates the energy of the whole solar system. The balance between Jupiter and the Sun holds the other planets in place.

Jupiter is the place where the man lays down his sword and his wand and the woman no longer spins the circle. The masculine and the feminine are no longer relevant. Here all is sexless. The male and the female become interchanging principles that function in the same being. It is the end of sex identity. To understand the great expanse of Jupiter, we become energy. We are no longer limited to the human form.

The 'letting go' exercise in chapter nine is particularly relevant to the process of moving through Jupiter.

Saturn

In the intensity of Saturn, the self disappears. In Saturn thought can only operate without an object. There is no longer identification. The thinker becomes the thought at the same time the thought becomes the thinker. We no longer say – "I see a rock", because "The rock sees I." Also, the tree is both the rock and I. I am the tree and the rock. The rock is the tree and me. The oneness of form becomes so transparent through the apparent separations on the surface. The tree is part of the rock and the rock is part of the human. The human is part of the ant, which is part of the buffalo. All is thought at once and at once there is all thought. Now the breath has to get deeper because words descend into nonsense. Here we cannot define because to define is to separate what is inseparable; you cannot talk about the rock without talking about the tree; you cannot talk about the human without talking about the ant. There are only incomplete sentences. The deeper you breathe into Saturn, the deeper the thought becomes, and the more obviously superficial is the word.

Exercise 27. **Wordless thought exercise**

Wordless thoughts can be reached through repetition exercises. Walking continuously in a circle around an object like a tree is a classic example. The Sun dance where the dancer paces towards and away from the tree, takes the dancer into a trance. Drumming for long periods or repeating the same sounds over and over also works. To undo the word maze of mind, absurd tasks can do the trick. Here are some examples.

Exercise One

Take of a sock from your left foot.
Put the sock on your right foot.
Take the sock off your right foot.
Put the sock on your left foot.
Continue for at least half an hour.

Exercise Two

Take two glasses. Fill one with orange juice, the other empty. Pause.

Pour the juice in the full glass to the empty glass. Pause.

Pour the juice in the full glass to the empty glass. Pause.

Repeat for half an hour.

It's a bit like a Samuel Beckett play. The states of mind one can reach during these exercises can be hypnotic.

Repeated movement exercises can also be very effective. This can help us also to bring our attention daily actions.

Exercise Three

Sit down.

Stand up.

Sit down.

Stand up.

How do you sit down? How do you stand up?

Repeat for ten minutes.

Exercise Four

A cup of tea.

Bring the cup to your mouth.

Put the cup back on the saucer.

How do you pick up the cup? How you put the cup back on the saucer?

Repeat for ten minutes.

You can try these exercises with your ordinary daily

movements around your living space —turning on the cooker, answering the phone, cleaning the floor, getting out of the bed, turning on the taps for a bath or shower, preparing a meal. What goes on in your mind whilst you are doing these things? The mind is often busy and chattering when we are not aware and listening.

Chiron

It is only from this speechless place that the healing power of Chiron can be understood. Chiron came from outside the solar system before it joined the movements of our planets around the Sun. Chiron brings the energy from outside. He is traditionally, the wounded healer. He is waiting to be healed before he can continue his journey. He heals himself through healing others.

The healing power of Chiron can be sung but not spoken. It can be vibrated through sound and through touch, but not

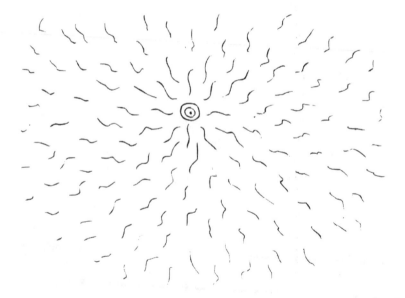

dissected into words. Colours may speak, but even they could not complete the tale. This energy is so subtle that we have to go deep into the wordless dream to touch it. It is a touch so subtle, one wonders if one has ever been loved before that moment.

Exercise 28. **Healing through Sound and Colour Vibration**

Everyone can sing. Everyone can make sound. This exercise is not an audition, you will not be judged on the quality of the sound that you make. In this exercise, we are attempting to find a sound vibration, which eases the energy flow through the chakras. This will balance the energy body.

Start with a breath awareness meditation.

When you are ready, take your attention to the base chakra. Feel the energy in the base chakra. Allow yourself to make a sound. It doesn't matter which sound. Any sound. Whilst you are making the sound, keep your attention on the base chakra. Let the sound evolve. Let the sound move wherever it feels to move, without taking your attention away from the base chakra.

When you feel you have connected with sound to the base chakra, move your attention to the second chakra. Repeat the sound exercise for this chakra.

Find a sound for each chakra, taking as much time as you need. This is likely to take more than one session. Also you may find that when you repeat the exercise, the sound for each chakra changes. Each sound is perfect for the moment in which it is made.

Once you have connected sound to the chakra areas, begin also to connect with colour. Whilst you are sounding around a chakra, see if you can connect with any colour. The colour may change, and there may be the same colours for different chakras.

Open your mind and body to sound and to colour.

Uranus

The generosity of Uranus allows the energy of Chiron and Merlin to enter our thought vibrations. It makes the uncontainable, containable. Its function is to make spaces so that the kind of energy in Chiron and Merlin can enter the bodies of the planets. It is also a kind of sieve, it cleans energy. It takes out the knots.

Imagine you are walking and in your mind you develop an argument with someone. It takes over your body and you move faster and faster. The energy of the argument pumps through your body and you might as well be walking on Mars for all you know; you don't notice anything around you. All of a sudden, you realise what's been going on. The fight has exhausted you. You need to sit down, take a rest, and let the argument go. Goodness – there is a tree! And there are birds! You are breathing! Seeing again! The walk continues at a slower, more enjoyable pace.

Uranus brings our attention to the blocks so that there is space for other energy to come in. Uranus brings our attention to our daily dramas, and then, as least we have the power to change channels, or even switch the whole television off.

Exercise 29. Slow Walking Meditation

Begin to walk very slowly. Walk in a circle. Notice the feeling of your feet, the balance of your body. As you are walking, watch your thoughts very carefully. As soon as you feel tension in your thoughts, stop. Breathe. Shake or move your body. Wait for the thoughts to calm. This may take a little while. When there is a little more space, begin to walk again.

Neptune and Pluto

Uranus is also the port for the great sea in the sky that is Neptune. The spaces expand even further than Jupiter. Neptune, although smaller in size, expands its energy out into the galaxy. Pluto is an island in the sea of Neptune. The dreaming body flows through these spaces like whales and dolphins that fly. The body expands into this great ocean of space and can now begin to stretch beyond the boundaries of the solar system. Only at Pluto, the last island in this mindset of planets, can we pause to take in the Sun. Pluto is the guardian of our solar system within time. It sees more space than any other planet in the solar system, and so it has a greater perspective. At Pluto, the Sun can be understood with the perspective of all the planets. The energies are integrated. The circles of the planets around the Sun star keep the space clear enough for the balance of the whole system to be held. The perspective of the twelve planetary centres connects in the conscious dream like an electrical circuit. The dreaming body is now connected to the power that will enable it to expand safely into the galaxy. The body of the solar system becomes the home base in this dream of space. It is our orientation in space. From here we can reach for the stars.

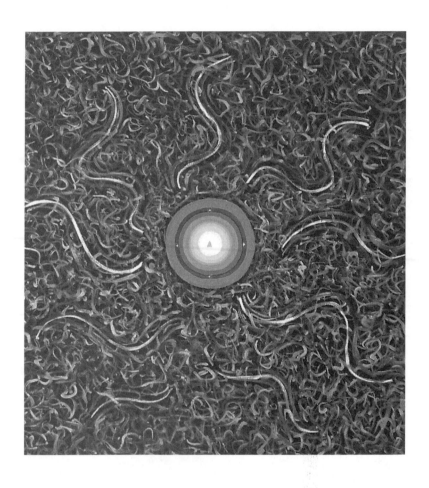

TWELVE - THE SUN

All things come from and came from the original breath, which was entirely free of intention. The tradition of enlightenment is the awareness of this primal breath, which is sometimes referred to as the luminous mind. It is a place of complete awareness. Although the dreamers became embroiled in their own projects, which some call karma, they were and still are close to the luminous mind of the original breath beyond time and space and separation. The human consciousness in general has to go through the mind spaces of the dreamers to retrace their steps to the breath of love: the giving without condition.

The closing of the human mind to this fluid interconnection through the medium of the crystal skulls, was the Earth aspect of the body afraid of losing itself. The kind of changes that were possible with this fluid interrelation was very exciting for the dreamers for whom the experiment of the human designers was really paying off. But the planet Earth in particular did not feel to move so fast. It was essentially afraid of its own death. Its fear was in fact well-founded because the cross-fertilisation of universal planetary information together with direct input of greater designer consciousness (dreaming from the position of the whole perspective of the universe), would have transformed the humans and planet Earth beyond recognition. The planet Earth self consciousness closed itself and therefore to some extent the minds of humans who were, after all, its children.

The dreamers had got themselves into a bit of a tangle. Their problem was that they were not perfect designers. In every breath of their experience, through their ideas and designs, was a part of the original breath, which had no intention. No matter how hard they held the focus of their attention on a particular idea, there would always be that spontaneous element of uncontrollable energy, which is entirely free of contingency. Everything they designed would to some extent develop its own will. This of course was as true of humans as well as the Earth, and the human will, because it has so much designer awareness, is capable of all kinds of fantastic schemes. There is a part of the human will that follows its Earth parent and there is a part of the human will that follows its designer parent, and there is a part of the human will that follows neither. The human spirit that wishes to be free could quite rightly describe itself as being caught between the will of the Earth to maintain itself and the will of the dreamers to evolve the dream through planetary interconnection. A lot of the human dream is an expression of the larger universal drama. It has to be said, however, that the designer consciousness (the power of the dreamers) is far far more powerful than Earth consciousness, and the dreamers could have their way without a moment's thought. But the planting of the first crystal seed and then the crystal skull was an involvement, and they couldn't transform the Earth against its will without pain to itself. The dreamers would rather the art of not always patient and gentle persuasion.

The human holds both dreamed Earth and dreamer designer consciousness, and so the human is an active medium between the two. At one time the human was a conscious active medium. The re-discovery of some physical quartz crystal skulls in the 20th century indicates that the Earth is ready for humans to take that role again. The rapid re-opening of the human mind to areas of consciousness that the human has not accessed for some time also indicates that there is a readiness for a new energetic dialogue. The human does have some say in all this. If the human really wants freedom, the human can contact the original breath through the physical experience of the breath in the body. It is technically possible to short circuit the whole of the history of the dream and return to the luminous mind of the beginning. But this, in one lifetime, is beyond almost all of us. The crystal skulls and the crystalline seed hold the information of the stages of consciousness from the place of the fixed idea (form) to the place of developing idea (design) to the place of no idea (breath). It is an extraordinary beautiful recapitulation. For most of us, it would seem to be our best chance of dreaming our own future.

The sun star is the eye of the dreamer

Klakiel (Four Arrows) is a Toltec elder with a very Aztec name. I met him in Brighton, England, of all places, where he was giving a lecture. He spoke of an experience he had in the desert where he was travelling with his students. They camped one night near a very small village of two or three houses, where the energy of the land is particularly powerful. At night, the stars were so clear, the group decided to do a ceremony to connect with them. To do this, they went to a high place away from the village. As they were standing, meditating, some young children came and stood behind them, watching whilst the elder and his students connected to the stars. The group felt very warm and all had the experience of a very clear energy passing through them, which made them feel very young and happy. They felt a sense of innocence and lightness. The children didn't stay long but long enough for the whole of the group to notice them.

The following day, Klakiel was talking to the people in the village about their experience in the ceremony, and he mentioned the children. He asked where they came from. There was only one young child in their family, and the nearest village was many miles away, and anyway, no mother would allow their children to wander so far away from home at night. Klakiel realised then that the children were the Star Children, something he had heard of in his tradition, but had not experienced until that moment. These children are healers. They heal from the place of innocence.

Some years later I was undertaking a series of meditations in Mexico taught to me by the Tibetan Dzogchen teacher Namkah Norbu. The exercises involve sitting still for long periods of time. The location is not important, in fact it can be anywhere. The important aspect of the exercise is sustained breathing in one position. I took this idea and put it together with a visit to a power point on the Oaxacan Pacific coast called Punta Cometa. It is a rock formation which projects like a pier into the sea. It faces due South and so looking out - the next stop is Antarctica. This great stretch of sea is one of the largest and deepest in the world. The depths are equivalent to the heights of the Himalayas.

I sat in one position, and looked out to sea, focusing on my breathing. I was allowing the vista to be my teacher. It was a beautiful teacher – pelicans diving into the sea, fish jumping, dolphins and whales. I am not sure if this is what Rimpoche had in mind in giving these exercises, but it was certainly enjoyable! I stayed in the same place the whole day, and as the Sun went down, I found myself attracted to look into it. I would look into it for a second or two before my eyes were overcome by its phenomenal light. I seemed to be trying to go through it with my attention. As the Sun set, I was able to sustain my gaze at the Sun, and I felt an incredible sense of peace. I watched as the sky gradually transformed through so many colours into the night. Gradually the stars appeared. It was easier to look into the stars than into the Sun, the stars were offering a different kind of energy. I felt a light tingling sensation in my body. I was on the end of the rock, and there was no one around, yet I could hear the playful laughter of children. Their energy came into my whole body, I felt so light, almost as if I wasn't there. The children touched my body with a kind of love that is pure play. They were offering the warmth of innocence. They laughed. I cried. This love I had forgotten. My body seemed to melt into the Earth and I surrendered. I could no longer hold any sitting position, I could only lay down and let the children heal me. They light up the eyes, and suddenly everything is possible again. Even love. Authentic. Real. Even love seems possible.

The following day I was drawn to go to a 'restaurant' I hadn't been to before. I say restaurant, but it was more like a

family living room. There was a typical Mexican set-up, the extended family sitting around several tables, a baby being swung in a hammock by his whistling brother, two young mothers holding their babies, lots of local chatter. Apart from the main group sat a child. She was clearly ill. I thought she was drugged. Whilst I ate, I watched her. There was something about her that called me. I believed she was autistic. I asked about her and I was told she was epileptic.

"Do you cure?" said one of the mothers.

It was a question out of the blue. I had worked with epileptics before in Mexico, mainly through massage and song to balance the energy body. I wouldn't call it a cure as such. I explained what I did. I offered to do a session with the child. They agreed.

During the session, the child barely moved. She would mumble occasionally words that were indecipherable. On the surface, it is very difficult with epileptics, particularly autistic epileptics, to know what effect, if any, the treatment has. Her mother was watching the whole while and wanted me to explain what was going on. As much as can be explained about these things, I told her that this child is sensitive and is open to frequencies of energies of which most of us are unaware. When most of us sleep, this child will be listening, and it is hard for the body to cope with all the information. Mercea Eliade writes that in ancient shamanic traditions, epilepsy was a sign of being connected to the sprits, and so epileptics were often also shamans. Indeed much of what our society calls 'mental illness' would have been acknowledged as special gifts in these tribes. This girl felt precious to me, a sensitive. I said to the mother -

"Ella es preciosa"

When I used this word "preciosa" the child looked me in the eyes for the first time. She smiled. I will never forget this moment. It was only for seconds, but long enough to feel what I had felt the night before under the stars. The Star Children spoke through this child and I knew in this moment that this child – so distant, so apart from the rest – was a gift to their family. I said to the mother that it is she, the child, who cures.

I went to see Chu-Ra to find out more about these experiences. She said to me directly –

"These are the children of the future and these are the children of the past." I didn't understand this but she wouldn't elaborate. She told me that now that they have contacted me, I should return to them. They will explain.

I did as Chu-Ra suggested, and I returned to the place where I first connected with the children. From then, over a period of years, I began to learn about the stars, and time.

Journey of the Soul

The soul spirals into the crystal centre of the Earth. It is a place charged with unimaginable energy. It is the charge that keeps the elemental circle turning; it is the charge that sustains the material world. The charge comes from outside the Earth planetary elemental circle. It comes from the Star. The Star is as close to the immediate force of the breath that the dreamer can get. It holds the process of the dreamer dreaming. The Star is the creative fire that designs and directs. It is practically immaterial. The rate of change in its fire is too fast for forms to be held there. They can only be held by projecting them out. Yet in the star, the forms are in the making, just like ideas grow in the human mind. Here is the inspiration. The Star is the place where something is about to become an idea.

The star is the strongest spirit of pure play. It comes from the very First Breath. The innocence of the Star Children are in themselves dreamforms of this sprit of play. The joy of play. Each star has the play of the animal. From the star it is possible to reach into the history and future of time –

There once was a lion that did not kill.

There once was a crocodile that had no teeth.

There once was a lion that wanted to find out what it was like to be a crocodile, and so the lion asked the crocodile to eat it.

The present manifestation of animal forms is a result of aeons of evolution. The closer they are to the original breath, the closer to home. There is no hunger. There is the luxury of play for the sake of play.

Animals will lead us home. In the desert, when I watch the shepherd taking the goats out to pasture on the touch scrub, and then I watch them bringing them back to his home, I feel it is the animal leading the man rather than the man leading the animal. This is how it is for us in the journey through the universal body. The animals hold the positions of the stars in the universe. They are the charts, the maps of the universe, and we have to understand animals to learn this most important journey of our lives — our death.

The human has to pass through all the animal stars because the human comes from the animal. The home of the human soul is not in any one Star. It is through all the stars to the other side of the dream. Our journey is through the composite animal game that brought us into the place of conception. To return to Soul, the human has to pass through the crystal centre and journey to the projector of energy itself. The dreamed meets the dreamer and passes even through this moment of birth. The circle of time starts from timelessness, and it is to timelessness that the soul returns.

THIRTEEN - TIMELESSNESS

Some years after listening at Punta Cometa, I started to receive information about time, which I couldn't understand. I went to see Chu-Ra and she said she would explain to me what they were talking about. For the first time in our eye to eye interaction, it was Chu-Ra who would be doing the talking. I was to listen and digest the information. She spoke in Spanish. Here is a translation, which is explained within the context of the twelve previous chapters.

"Time moves both clockwise and anti-clockwise. Before time and after time is timelessness. The movement is best shown in a diagram. (Chu-Ra drew this simple diagram):

Timelessness

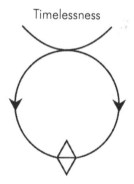

The beginning is the end and the end is the beginning. The future is the past and the past is the future. The halfway mark is the double pyramid, the time of the ancient Egyptian and Mexican civilisations. We have passed the half way mark and are now moving toward the end.

The characteristic of the end is the same as the beginning. It is nearer the first breath; nearer timelessness; nearer innocence; nearer to energy without condition. Hunger decreases the nearer we approach Soul (in timelessness).

The further we move to the end, the further we move away from duality – material, immaterial; good, evil; pain, pleasure; masculine, feminine; life, death; future, past. The dualities dissolve, the forms become more fluid like clouds or water. We move towards (return to) the innocence of play.

The whole movement of time is the release of fixed attention. The double pyramid era was the time when the dream was most fixed in the attention of the dreamers. The dreamers try and sustain their attention in this time bubble of the pyramid era for as long as possible. They try and create the illusion of timelessness within time, but it cannot be sustained. Time is always movement to and from timelessness. From the pyramid point in time, the fixed attention was not and is not so strong."

To show me how this works, Chu-Ra took me to Tula, an ancient pyramid city North of Mexico City. She sat down with her back to one of the Atlantids – twelve-foot high carved statues of the ancient priests. She told me to sit down and look into her eyes. She told me to read his eyes.

I felt lost. I didn't know what to look for. Yet even through I had no sense of what to see, I was being 'seen', by Chu-Ra. I felt she was drawing me into her eyes and I had a sensation of falling. I was moving into spaces I had never been to before. Spaces without space, it seemed, I had no sense of where my body began or ended. Yet time was present. I felt time in the sense of growing older, growing older into the future and yet growing older into the past. I felt I was falling into the spaces of my ancestors who were also my children. They were directing me through this dreamspace in a very particular way. I let go. Surrendered to their movement. They took me to a very specific realm. I was at Tula, and the priests were performing a ceremony.

The priests turned around and saw me. Immediately, they covered their faces and ran at me. I felt like they were going to kill me.

"Don't move!" Chu-Ra was talking to me through her eyes. "They can't hurt you."

True enough, they ran towards me and through me, as if I was a phantom.

The scene changed. The priests were doing very ordinary things it seemed. They were aware of me, I felt, but tried to ignore me.

"Try and catch the eyes," said Chu-Ra.

I tried to look into their eyes, but every time I walked up to one, he looked away.

"Patience." said Chu-Ra. "Stay in the scene."

I don't know how long I stayed in that place. It felt like many years. I felt like I had been doing nothing more in my life than wait for one of them to 'see' me. It was as if they wanted to look at me, but they dare not do so. It seemed a huge effort for them to ignore me.

Eventually one gave way. He looked at my eyes and Chu-Ra caught them. The priest 'fell' into my eyes like my eyes were a sink. With one they all followed. The priests fell out of the scene and through the journey of time I had travelled. They came out of my body and I jumped. Chu-Ra was still there, looking at me.

"What happened?" I said.

"They have gone into the Sun."

"This is the trick of the dreamers, to hold themselves in time." said Chu-Ra. "Yet no matter how perfect the dream, time is always illusory. They could not sustain their illusion with me in their dream. Once they knew their time was up, they had to die the perfect death. They understood they were dreamed and the illusion in which they was trapped. From there on there was only one thing to do – to fall into timelessness."

"As soon as they came through your body, they went straight for the Sun. They knew what was happening. They resisted in their dream, but they couldn't hold the tension of their illusion. It only needed one of them because they were all depending on the others to hold the time in a grip. As soon as one let go, the others wanted to follow. This is difficult to understand. They resist, and want to stay in the illusion for fear of the unknown. But when they see the chance of freedom, they want to fly. It is like a prisoner who would try and convince you how beautiful is their prison, and yet secretly yearns to be released."

For me this opened up a dream of understanding. I understood in that moment that all repeated behavioural patterns are like these prisons of time. I understood that healing is to release ourselves from our own time prisons. We hold onto our past patterns because it is all that we know. It is our security, yet secretly we yearn for someone to open the door. It is the fear of freedom.

Chu-Ra continued to explain – "All forms are made of the repetitions of fixed attention. The material world is made of circles of repeated experience. They are tiny circles in time, which hold the object in place. As time increases (decreases) beyond the elastic limit of the pyramid era, the circles of attention are gradually released in the recapitulation."

"At the end of formation is non-formation. We move towards the blinding energy of timelessness. This energy is blinding because it cannot be seen. It cannot be known, it cannot be designed. It is beyond the scope of any dreamer's mind, beyond imagination, beyond thought. The pure energy of Soul is the energy of known unknowing. Nothing can be known - which is the knowing.

For the Earth planet, the gradual acceleration (deceleration) into timelessness is the crystal energy moving more into the surface. The anti-clockwise spin moves through the surface of the Earth until there is no clockwise elemental spin to maintain. When the clockwise spin dissolves, the crystal also dissolves; the circles spin into space, the material becomes immaterial."

I found this difficult to understand, this notion of time being clockwise and anti-clockwise, so Chu-Ra told me to look into her eyes. I understood there and then that it doesn't mean that the film of history is reversed. Time is not a linear concept. I understood through her eyes that it is the gradual loosening of fixed attention, where forms become more fluid. It is like being able to breathe the return to the fluid centre of the Sun.

"At present we are experiencing acceleration on this planet, and this is causing panic." said Chu-Ra. "The pace of change increases and there is less to hold onto. This makes people hold on more."

"The best we can do," she said, "is to let go of knowing. Let go of planning, let go of anticipating, let go of designing. Trust in the mystery. This is our best security. Time will not wait. We are going home."

This is the curious pain of ecstasy. To love is to let go. A long kiss and the Earth literally moves. We forget where we are, but it doesn't matter. Delicious foolishness – we are in love.

APPENDIX: SPEAK

We start at the beginning. First Breath. Without intention. An exhalation. No thought. By itself. It began. Breath of no thing. Natural. Nothing itself. There is no difference.

An inhalation. Appearing different. From no breath to breath. But there was no intention. It was nothing. It still is nothing.

And then the catch. This energy. To catch the energy of the first breath. And make something. The dreamers. To take this energy – entirely nothing, entirely free of intention – and use it for something. The possibilities are endless. What would it be like?

The dreamers. They came after the initial breath. They came from the breath. But they were different from the pure breath. Because they had intention. They had big ideas. Plans. The original breath is free of care. It does not have any intention. It is the essence of nothing. But the dreamers want to make something of it.

What were the first experiments? Half forms. Playing. Appearance and disappearance. A hint of a possibility. Shapes that never quite stick, fluidity; a stream of the consciousness of beginnings. The magicians starting from scratch.

What do they learn? Light and darkness. Two tones. The one makes the other. Difference. And space. Continuum. Limitation. Boundary. Form.

To keep the image still, they have to concentrate. To hold something in place requires focus. The dreamers learn how to make a decision. They discover time. This is it. Even if it is for a second. A form needs time to exist, or it is lost in the continuum. The more time that is given to the form, the more fixed it can become. The dreamers have to learn to focus. And then they can make something. Even if it is only for a second.

Concept of time. Concept of space. Concept of difference.

These are the basic starting places of the magicians. And then they get clever. They discover the differences in light. They discover colour. They discover differences in darkness. They discover depth. Perspective. Spaces within spaces. And then the masterstroke. Volume. The possibility of the third dimension. The object. The object in perspective. The dreamers get very excited. They play around with all kinds of holograms. They are fantastic with their image nation. There is no limitation to the design possibilities. But this is still the drawing board. There is still a sense of preparation. Soon they would have to learn how to focus with greater concentration. They wanted to learn how to make something that matters, something more than just an idea and a possibility. They discovered the elements. Still from the same original breath. They discovered how to transform breath into air, the speed of air into fire, then hot slowing to cold, gas - gas can congest into rock or condense into water. It was a magical time. The dreamers made huge discoveries. And all from the breath of nothing. They couldn't believe their luck.

Space, time, light, shadow, the third dimension and now the elements. The experiments really could begin. They worked with extremes at first, extremes of fire, extremes of earth; they make planets and stars over and again, practising with various gradients of the elements, but to a large extent they do not know what they are doing, they do not have complete control. Just as the breath of nothing has no control over the designers of the breath, so the designers of the breath have little control over their designs. The elements are such big principles; they have a sense of their own law, which the dreamers understood in theory but not in practise. Each star and each planet was the attempt by the dreamers to get a clearer idea of how the elements actually work. In time, they learn, and so these novice chemists and physicists begin to develop the possibility of balance. It was all about focus again. By holding planets in certain rotations they could create fields of energy that would remain in place. It is like creating a context, or a background, and they found a way to hold their focus long enough to explore further possibilities. So in our solar system, for example, the dreamers are holding the focus of planets orbiting one central star. This has the effect of creating various fields of energy, which have a certain consistency in which other life forms can thrive. This system of our star sun was by no means the first with which the dreamers developed this type of attention. It is an idea that they had been developing through many repetitions, and each repetition in infinity gave them a chance to perfect their idea.

The planets and stars were like the stage set of the dreamers' play. They developed through numerous design stages an elemental principle that enabled them to experiment with various forms. Their first experiments were very simple and kept very close to the essence of the four essential elements. But as they developed in skills, they could make increasingly complex creatures, and on a planet such as Earth, which was one of their better constructions, they could play with all kinds of ideas. But in order to develop further, the dreamers had to do something they hadn't done before. Up to this point they had treated the universe like their own laboratory, and they always had a certain distance in their attitude. They were essentially observers of phenomenon. But they could see that this separation of observer and observed, was something of a limitation. They realised that in order to go further, they had to invest a part of themselves in what they were creating. To some extent, they had to become what they were designing. In some of their more developed creations, they planted a seed of their own consciousness. This seed was made of crystal.

The dreamers chose crystal to hold the seed of their consciousness because it was of form and not of form at the same time. They had designed crystal to grow into a very strong structure, yet despite its strength of focus into form; it could hold all the hologramatic thoughts of the dreamers' early days. It could hold the traces of the connections between thoughts right back to the first impulse to design. In short, crystal had the capacity to store the complete history of thought from the first breath. Moreover, it could continue to store all the development of thought from the seed of the designer's consciousness.

What the dreamers did was to risk part of themselves in their own creation. They planted seeds of themselves in every planet in which they had a particular interest without giving themselves entirely away. They made themselves into the subject as well as the object; the observed as well as the observer; the experiment as well as the experimenters. They were completely involved in a way they had never been before.

From the perspective of the planets, this injection of the seed into their centre was like the Gods coming to land. In terms of planet Earth mythology it was like an alien invasion. It was alien because the Earth had never been touched before by the hand of its creator. It had only really been a material thought projection of a developed idea. But the dreamers wanted to touch what they had made. They wanted to experience what it is like to be made of the elements. From now on, the dreamers would have to experience everything that they conceived. So they began to take more care.

The first masterstroke of the crystalline designer seeds was the discovery of the principle elemental construction: DNA. With this principle, itself a seed, the dreamers in the planets could extend themselves into various forms whilst the larger part of the dreamer's consciousness could observe the results. The observer could feed the results of its discoveries to the developing dream of the crystalline seed. In this way, they had the joint perspectives of inside and outside.

The first extensions of the crystal seed were understandably tentative: Simple plants, grasses, microbes, amoebas. But gradually the extensions became more daring – trees, insects, fish, and eventually reptiles and mammals. But at every stage of the breath from the very beginning, no energy could control entirely its own effect. As the first breath could not control the dreamers, the dreamers could not control the design, and now the design seed could not control its own growth. It tried to stabilise its ideas through repetition, and with some of its earlier concepts, this was successful, particularly with grasses and insects. But as it developed more compound extensions, so also it had to develop the truth of energy feeding on itself. Some parts of the crystal life would feed on other parts. It created new problems of balance within the planetary body. The seed saw in itself this dangerous yet necessary principle of growth. This was particularly difficult to control. The dinosaurs were the most extreme example of energy bodies that had grown too big for the main body to balance. It is said that a comet's collision with the planet Earth altered the elemental conditions to such an extent that the dinosaurs could no longer exist. But this was really a crude example of designer consciousness attempting to reassert some kind of control over its own body. Although the dinosaurs were a product of its seed, it was a product that had taken too much of a hungry will of its own and threatened to dominate the other aspects of the seeds' growth. It was a mark of how strong the dinosaurs had become that the larger aspects of design consciousness would go to such lengths in order to change so radically the surface of one of its planetary inheritances (investments.)

Which brings us to another problem for the dreamers. Although they conceived of the planets, and were responsible for the principles under which they evolved, they could not control the planetary evolution itself. The planets had already evolved their own sense of innate movement, which was beyond the direct control of the dreamers. So when the dreamers took the step of injecting their seed into the planets, they were to some extent inheriting a body which already had an independent history. So much of the problems experienced by the seed of the dreamers were in trying to understand the planetary body in which it was planted. The dreamers were very imperfect magicians who did not have full control over their own magic. The dinosaurs were a gross result of the dreamers' crystal seed attempting to combine effectively with the elemental planetary body. The sudden and dramatic demise of the dinosaurs, together with every other species that has overstepped the mark of the dreamers' will, is well preserved in the memory of the planetary body.

The main tension between the planet Earth and the crystal design seed is one of pace. The dreamers always want to go faster than the planet because essentially the dreamers think before they feel. (The planet was after all originally designed by the same consciousness that seeks a greater pace of change.) The Earth has its own way and its own time, and it suffers all the fall-out from the dreamers' experiments. It has to absorb the principle of death, which allows the dreamers to keep trying. The dreamers have a problem because the various individual parts, which grow from the crystal seed, do not have the same vision as the seed itself. The creations of the dreamers are not willing to be merely part of a grand experiment. They value their life for its self. The planet itself also only knew its own life; it did not have the external presence of the dreamers whose consciousness extended into all aspects of the universe. So the pain absorbed by the planet would always be far greater than the dreamers who could still jump outside to the relative indifference of the observer.

These were some of the problems facing the dreamers. To deal with them, they invested more of their energy into the planet. They came, as it were, a second time, and planted a seed within the first seed that had developed into all the various forms thus far. Their intention this time was to make a mirror, something that would reflect themselves more completely so they could experience life on Earth to a greater depth. This time they planted more crystal, but a particular crystal with a particular energy. They planted the crystal skull.

The crystal skull was the birth of humanity. From the intention of the form planted in the planet, the human would develop through its various forms into a body that could hold the memory of the dreamers themselves. The dreamers in planting the crystal skull had sown the seed for the manifestation of their own reflection to be born on this planet. The human would not only come from the seed, but would develop the same awareness as the seed itself. The intention with the placing of the crystal skull was to make designed humans as human designers. The dreamers wanted to see themselves on Earth.

When the dreamers first invested themselves with the crystal seed into the planets, they had to learn the exact fruits of their actions. The elemental base that they had consciously dreamt was by today's standards incredibly crude, and if they wanted to develop further possibilities from the base, they had to modify and refine their original bold and brash elemental concoction. Because they chose to become part of the planet, they had to develop the notion of care. When the dreamers originally projected their ideas into a mind space, they created an outside; they created something that appeared to be outside themselves. The original breath, of which they were part, was all of one mind, but as soon as they began designing, they created mind spaces within the one mind, which had the appearance, at least, of being outside. Even the act of seeing in order to design required the dreamers to develop notions of mindspace outside space and mindspace inside, even though they knew it was the same. By entering into the planet, they entered with their inside mind space into an outside mind space, which for them was a great lesson. It was a lesson in empathy. The dreamers had to learn compassion. They had to learn how to feel, to sense the thing outside, which even though was their own conception, was to some extent alien to them because it was for so long during the huge time spaces of elemental experimentation, outside of their direct experience.

Conversely, the planet, which before had only been part of the experiment of elemental evolution, was now seeing itself for the first time through the eyes of the dreamers. This meeting of the inside mind space with the outside mind space; of the designers with the designed; the dreamers with the dreamt, was the first stage in the development of self. Of awareness of the self. The self of the universe was in dialogue with its own material; within the whole mind, the dreamers developed a sense of the planetary selves within it. There was relation. There was relationship.

Everything had to change. The planet could no long continue to simply move wherever the laws of the elements would take them. The dreamers were trying to do something more – they were trying to co-ordinate a creative movement. They had seen the possibility of evolution. And this required co-operation.

The essential problem for the dreamers was that the things they had created through the focusing of their attention were now so focused in their attention that it wasn't easy to change. When there was only mind space, it was easy for them to simply project an idea, and see what happened. But as they learnt to focus their attention with more concentration, the forms of their concen-tration became more stable. The planets themselves were made up of elemental principles, energetic movements that obeyed certain laws. These laws of energy themselves were projections of the dreamers' thoughts which themselves were necessary for the elemental planetary experiments to develop. When the dreamers' planted the crystal seed of consciousness in the planet, they inherited their own laws. They had to learn to work within the energetic principles of their own projections, which for them was an incredible limitation. The crystal seed had the consciousness of change and design within the laws of its greater consciousness. The impulse of the pure designer energy is to move and develop, and the impulse of the planetary energy is to hold the attention of its laws so that it can continue to exist. It is the tension of the radical and the conservative.

The history of the evolution of man is essentially the gradual awakening of the human Earth body to its own dreamer. All religions were stylised forms of the same intention – to connect with the (God/Goddess) designer consciousness in the rest of the universe. Because there are crystal skulls in all of the planets in our solar system, astrological understanding was a hugely important part of this re-connection. There was a point in the development of human consciousness at the time of the ancient Egyptian and earlier cultures of Mexico in particular, when the crystal skull connections between the planets were an integrated part of the spiritual life. Important decisions would be made in accordance with the balancing of the 13 planetary centres of the solar system. This balanced ring of 13 allowed the consciousness of humanity to open to other areas of the universe where the designer consciousness is planted in other planets, and where the designer consciousness is still an observer and closer to the original breath.

The human mind was so open at this time that it was possible for the objective designer consciousness to feed the crystal skull seeds directly using the humans as mediums. This gave certain humans great power, which was at times abused. It was also possible for the design consciousness to cross-fertilise its ideas that had developed from one planet to another. Again the crystal skull was a powerful enough medium to affect this transition. This movement of energy would again, in human mythology, be an alien landing, but really it was just a connection of one part of the universal one mind to another part. Different planets and star systems in the universe have different aspects of experience, and the dreamers seek a union and interconnection of this experience. It is difficult for a planet to understand its connection with other parts of the whole when it can only see itself in its own context.

It must be remembered that all things come from and came from the original breath, which was entirely free of intention. The tradition of enlightenment is the awareness of this primal breath, which is sometimes referred to as the luminous mind. It is a place of complete awareness. Although the dreamers became embroiled in their own projects, which some call karma, they were and still are close to the luminous mind of the original breath beyond time and space and separation. The human consciousness in general has to go through the mind spaces of the dreamers to retrace their steps to the breath of love: the giving without condition.

The closing of the human mind to this fluid interconnection through the medium of the crystal skulls, was the Earth aspect of the body afraid of losing itself. The kind of changes that were possible with this fluid interrelation was very exciting for the dreamers for whom the experiment of the human designers was really paying off. But the planet Earth in particular did not feel to move so fast. It was essentially afraid of its own death. Its fear was in fact well-founded because the cross-fertilisation of universal planetary information together with direct input of greater designer consciousness (dreaming from the position of the whole perspective of the universe), would have transformed the humans and planet Earth beyond recognition. The planet Earth self consciousness closed itself and therefore to some extent the minds of humans who were, after all, its children.

The dreamers had got themselves into a bit of a tangle. Their problem was that they were not perfect designers. In every breath of their experience, through their ideas and designs, was a part of the original breath, which had no intention. No matter how hard they held the focus of their attention on a particular idea, there would always be that spontaneous element of uncontrollable energy, which is entirely free of contingency. Everything they designed would to some extent develop its own will. This of course was as true of humans as well as the Earth, and the human will, because it has so much designer awareness, is capable of all kinds of fantastic schemes. There is a part of the human will that follows its Earth parent and there is a part of the human will that follows its designer parent, and there is a part of the human will that follows neither. The human spirit that wishes to be free could quite rightly describe itself as being caught between the will of the Earth to maintain itself and the will of the dreamers to evolve the dream through planetary interconnection. A lot of the human dream is an expression of the larger universal drama. It has to be said, however, that the designer consciousness (the power of the dreamers) is far far more powerful than Earth consciousness, and the dreamers could have their way without a moment's thought. But the planting of the first crystal seed and then the crystal skull was an involvement, and they couldn't transform the Earth against its will without pain to itself. The dreamers would rather the art of not always patient and gentle persuasion.

The human holds both dreamed Earth and dreamer designer consciousness, and so the human is an active medium between the two. At one time the human was a conscious active medium. The re-discovery of some physical quartz crystal skulls in the 20th century indicates that the Earth is ready for humans to take that role again. The rapid re-opening of the human mind to areas of consciousness that the human has not accessed for some time also indicates that there is a readiness for a new energetic dialogue. The human does have some say in all this. If the human really wants freedom, the human can contact the original breath through the physical experience of the breath in the body. It is technically possible to short circuit the whole of the history of the dream and return to the luminous mind of the beginning. But this, in one lifetime, is beyond almost all of us. The crystal skulls and the crystalline seed hold the information of the stages of consciousness form the place of the fixed idea (form) to the place of developing idea (design) to the place of no idea (breath). It is an extraordinary beautiful recapitulation. For most of us, it would seem to be our best chance of dreaming our own future.

EXERCISES

Centre of the Conscious Dream

Desert of Mexico

Courses also in the U.S. and Europe and by Internet

www.12consciousdreamers.com

BOOKS

O is a symbol of the world, of oneness and unity. In different cultures it also means the "eye," symbolizing knowledge and insight. We aim to publish books that are accessible, constructive and that challenge accepted opinion, both that of academia and the "moral majority."

Our books are available in all good English language bookstores worldwide. If you don't see the book on the shelves ask the bookstore to order it for you, quoting the ISBN number and title. Alternatively you can order online (all major online retail sites carry our titles) or contact the distributor in the relevant country, listed on the copyright page.

See our website **www.o-books.net** for a full list of over 500 titles, growing by 100 a year.

And tune in to myspiritradio.com for our book review radio show, hosted by June-Elleni Laine, where you can listen to the authors discussing their books.

mySpiritRadio